Climbing to the moon by
The Eels

Steal This Music

D0886406

Steal This Music

HOW INTELLECTUAL PROPERTY LAW

AFFECTS MUSICAL CREATIVITY

Joanna Demers

THE UNIVERSITY OF GEORGIA PRESS

ATHENS AND LONDON

© 2006 by the University of Georgia Press

Athens, Georgia 30602

All rights reserved

Designed by Kathi Dailey Morgan & Anne Richmond Boston

Set in Electra by Bookcomp

Printed and bound by Maple-Vail

The paper in this book meets the guidelines for permanence
and durability of the Committee on Production Guidelines
for Book Longevity of the Council on Library Resources.

Printed in the United States of America

06 07 08 09 10 C 5 4 3 2 1

06 07 08 09 10 P 5 4 3 2 1

Library of Congress Cataloging-in-Publication Data

Demers, Joanna Teresa, 1975–

Steal this music : how intellectual property

law affects musical creativity / Joanna Demers.

p. cm.

Includes bibliographical references and index.

ISBN-13: 978-0-8203-2710-5 (hardcover : alk. paper)

ISBN-10: 0-8203-2710-7 (hardcover : alk. paper)

ISBN-13: 978-0-8203-2777-8 (pbk. : alk. paper)

ISBN-10: 0-8203-2777-8 (pbk. : alk. paper)

1. Copyright—Music—United States. 2. Composition
(Music) 3. Intellectual property—United States. I. Title.

KF3035.D46 2006   346.7304'82—dc22   2005021226

British Library Cataloging-in-Publication Data available

CONTENTS

MAKING MUSIC IN THE
SOUNDSCAPES OF THE LAW

Although copyright applies to many cultural expressions, its extension into the field of musical creativity manifests most clearly the complexities of the law and the range of its cultural influence. From its origins as a right to prohibit the unauthorized copying of sheet music, musical copyright has dramatically expanded. With respect to musical compositions, the law now enables copyright holders to enjoin public performances, broadcasting, the making of sound recordings in any medium, and, in many jurisdictions, the sharing of music with the aid of digital technology. Each of these exclusive rights can be separately assigned or multiply licensed for distinct purposes, potentially creating tangled webs of prohibition that freight the use of music with dangers of litigation. More and more performances are now considered public (for example, songs sung at family meals in restaurants, at children's day care centers, and at summer camps), and the reproduction of even short samples of a song is potentially an infringement if the original work is recognizable.

The reach of copyright law has extended far beyond compositions to encompass sound recordings and performances as unique "works" of creativity deserving protection. Rights over recordings and performances, known as neighboring rights, in many jurisdictions are simply incorporated into existing copyright statutes. They exacerbate the already complicated webs of protection woven around musical works. Terms of copyright protection have become progressively longer, ensuring that fewer and fewer works of musical creativity enter the public domain. The realm of acts exempt from infringement liability—including certain reproductions, performances, and communications of musical works—has not expanded as rapidly as the body of limitations that increasingly encroach upon the range of social activities in which music may be enjoyed. Even the physical media for fixing music have been taxed, and legislators have passed laws against circumventing technological "locks" used to prevent copying of electronic media even where some of the copying the new laws prevent might actually be permitted under traditional copyright laws. Although there is a rich body of case law elaborating the public's right to fair dealing and fair use of works, copyright owners seek to circumvent it. In any case, however potentially generous, fair use is valuable only to those who can afford the fees necessary for aggressive litigation. Most fans and creators who share music will be sufficiently intimidated by a corporate "cease-and-desist letter" on legal letterhead to stop their offending activity—regardless of how creative, transformative, noncommercial, or noncompetitive it may be—go underground, or pay a licensing fee set by corporate fiat. Meanwhile, the recording industry that tends to control the greatest concentration of copyrights in musical works has also learned to deploy contract law, trademark law, common law unfair competition suits, and even publicity rights to limit listening practices and creative use of music without authorization and payment.

This legal situation leaves us with a musical culture structured primarily in favor of the financial interests of corporate intellectual property holders and shaped by the contractual conditions they establish. Any presumption that music serves public purposes and helps support social objectives seems to have vanished just as any notion that the state should act to protect the public interest and to secure access to a range of public goods has become illegitimate. Even the long tradition of socializing the next generation into society's norms and values through music is rendered suspect when underfunded school systems and nonprofit social groups must pay royalties to pass down a nation's cultural heritage to its children.

The irony here is that perhaps no area of human creativity relies more heavily upon appropriation and allusion, borrowing and imitation, sampling and intertextual commentary than music, nor any area where the mythic figure of the creative genius composing in the absence of all external influence is more absurd. Contemporary technologies have greatly multiplied and democratized opportunities for musical creativity and self-expression, while also providing means for the musically enthusiastic to share music with others and to accelerate the processes of collaboration on which musical innovation relies. Have we reached a crossroads? Will the ever more aggressive legal tactics of corporate intellectual property holders put an end to sharing and collaboration, or is there a "will to music" that will continue to energetically evade attempts to restrict such practices?

In this lively and accessible primer, Joanna Demers explores this terrain and moves considerably beyond it, demonstrating that the intellectual property provisions that apply to music do not merely prohibit forms of musical expression and modes of consumption. Through interpretation and misinterpretation by creators and users, intellectual property rights in music help shape the field of musical forms available to us, the tendencies of musical allusion and appropriation, and the emergence of alternative forms of regulation and musical sociality. From a sociological and anthropological perspective, intellectual property law is generative as well as prohibitive.[1] Creative practices and new norms, values, and conventions—new moral economies—grow up in the shadows of the law.

The privileging of melody in the law's recognition of the musical work, for example, may shape practices of arrangement. The availability of materials in the public domain may attract disproportionate creative investments in older tunes. In the mid-twentieth century, three conditions contributed to an environment conducive to forms of musical appropriation that gave birth to rock 'n' roll: first, the law's failure to recognize unfixed works from oral traditions; second, the limited protection afforded sound recordings and their performers; and third, the lack of acknowledgment of voice and performance styles as legally protectable attributes. The law's validation of melody and harmony as protectable entities has arguably provoked forms of avant-garde musical collage that highlight "the arbitrary distinctions between sound, music, and noise" as Demers reveals. Social resistance to the legal equivalent of musical composers and literary authors is expressed in forms of creative transformation that challenge the hegemony of authorial intention in determining musical significance. The novelty collages ("mash-ups") that Demers considers owe a great deal of their popularity to their illegality and to the creative ways in which authorial personas that enjoy increasing protection by intellectual property laws are drawn into new realms of unintended signification. Her reading of the evolution of allusion and sampling practices in hip-hop and "esoteric collage" is an insightful exploration of the distinctive means by which the performance of authenticity in a cultural tradition demands forms of cultural appropriation suppressed by the overreaching of copyright holders.

This volume is an important study of shifting cultural values and new musical practices generated in relation to a legal climate characterized by uncertainty and change. Compositional collage activity appears to be strongly influenced by the copyright status of musical materials, and new technologies are evolving to enable musicians to render collages whose musical origins cannot be discerned. A new market in "pre-cleared" samples has developed to meet creative demand. New social venues for sampling, such as underground parties and scratch competitions, have emerged to evade legal constraints. The growing role of copyright in the field of music has also turned an increasing number of artists into intellectual property activists, just as it has spawned an alternative, more democratic regulatory regime—the Creative Commons, in which creators and users bypass corporate middlemen to ensure that music is available for shared use.

World music also continues to "constitute an ethical minefield," as Demers admits, because of the weak protection afforded to non-Western musical traditions and the sense that profiting from the musical forms of others is exploitative. This situation is likely to change in the near future as new forms of intellectual property protection are devised for "traditional cultural expressions" and as digital communications technologies make it easier or more likely that communities of origin will become aware of unauthorized appropriations of their musical heritage. If these new cultural rights are exercised by governments, however, it seems likely that the controls they exercise and the fees they demand will be resented as much as those of their corporate counterparts. In this case as well, I suspect, we will discover that the practices, values, and meanings shaped in the light of the law and in its shadows will be as diverse as the forms of musical creativity we celebrate.

Rosemary Coombe
Canada Research Chair in Law, Communication,
and Culture, York University

NOTE

1. Coombe, *The Cultural Life of Intellectual Properties.*

ACKNOWLEDGMENTS

At every stage of this project, I have been blessed with generous colleagues who helped make this book a reality. For their thoughtful critiques and advice, I thank Anupam Chander, Mary Francis, Paul Geller, Nancy Guy, Chris Johnstone, Dan Klerman, Lawrence Lessig, Kembrew McLeod, Paul Saint-Amour, Ellen Seiter, Siva Vaidhyanathan, and the participants and contributors of the 2004 Interdisciplinary Law and Humanities Workshop at UCLA. For their willingness to be interviewed, I thank Matt Baldoni, DJ Rob Fatal, Dr. Wulf, Mark Goldstein, Derrick Finch, Judith Finell, David Hunt, Paul Lansky, John Oswald, Juliana Snapper, and John Wall. I also thank the University of Georgia Press and particularly Andrew Berzanskis for guiding this project with such panache. I am grateful to Rosemary Coombe and to the anonymous readers, whose comments were invaluable. The research for this book was supported by a grant from the James H. Zumberge Faculty Research and Innovation Fund at the University of Southern California, and I thank my colleagues in USC's Flora L. Thornton School of Music for their intellectual and moral support.

For their generosity, I owe a great deal to my friends and professors at Princeton University, especially Scott Burnham, Nicola Gess, Wayne Heisler, Simon Morrison, and Scott Paulin. Lynn Itagaki has

inspired me with her writing since we were in the sixth grade together, and every writer should be lucky enough to have her as a
friend. My parents Jim and Joan and my brother Dana have been
generous and encouraging throughout my life, and never more than
the moment when I announced my harebrained plans to become a
musicologist. I dedicate this book to my beloved husband Inouk.

INTRODUCTION

On July 15, 2003, an MTV Online article announced that the heavy metal supergroup Metallica had filed a lawsuit against a Canadian group named Unfaith. According to author Joe D'Angelo, Metallica accused Unfaith of using E chords followed by F chords without permission, a harmonic progression that Metallica claimed to have trademarked. MTV posted a link to Metallica's Web site, in which bandleader Lars Ulrich defended the suit as justifiable protection of the band's distinctive sound. The D'Angelo article received more than two hundred thousand hits within the first two days of its posting and became a hot topic of conversation for several Internet discussion groups. Responses to the allegations ranged from incredulity to outrage. The story was a sign that something (Metallica, the music industry, or lawyers) had abused intellectual property laws originally designed to prevent musical plagiarism.

But by July 17, 2003, Court TV and CNN announced that the lawsuit was a hoax constructed by Erik Ashley, the singer-songwriter behind Unfaith. To the embarrassment of the agencies that reported the D'Angelo story, Ashley admitted he had posted articles on his own Web site, 411mania, that appeared as if they had been published on the MTV and Metallica Web sites. Sincerely or otherwise, Ashley claimed that he didn't intend for the story to be taken seriously but meant it only as a satire of Metallica's notoriously litigious behavior. The story seemed plausible enough, however, to be reported by National Public Radio, MSNBC, and *Rolling Stone.*

Chord changes that are based on the E–F pattern are found in compositions throughout the world; in music theory, there is a term to describe this particular sound: the Phrygian progression. You've heard Phrygian progressions if you've listened to flamenco or to Georges Bizet's opera *Carmen.* The Phrygian sound also characterizes pieces from the Baroque period in Western classical music as well as traditional music of the Middle East. To draw an analogy to language, Metallica's alleged charge is akin to a writer's trademarking all words in which the letter F follows the letter E simply because the author often uses words containing that letter combination.

This hoax was believable because it seemed to confirm consumer suspicions about both Metallica and the entertainment industry. Prior to this, in April 2000 Metallica had sued Napster for misappropriating the band's copyrighted material. At the time, Napster still functioned as a free file-sharing service. But because Napster only facilitated, rather than initiated, file transfers, it claimed that it was not responsible if users distributed unauthorized copies of recordings. By 2000 many in the music business condemned Napster for abusing songwriters and performers, but only a few artists like Metallica dared to confront the company directly. Identifying more than three hundred thousand private individuals who had exchanged the band's music without permission, Metallica demanded that Napster block these users from accessing the file-sharing service. Other stars like rapper Dr. Dre eventually filed similar suits. Yet because Metallica launched the first attack, the band weathered invective from music fans who believed they had a right to free file sharing. This resentment was particularly acute because Metallica lyrics describe alienation from consumer culture. Censuring fans and their preferred means of acquiring music undercut Metallica's credibility, suggesting that the band was actually complicit with the very things it condemned.

The case against Napster was only one of several lawsuits Metallica filed to protect itself from commercial exploitation. Between 1999 and 2001 the band brought suit against three companies (Victoria's Secret, Neiman Marcus, and MHT Luxury Alloys) that used "Metallica" as a brand name for their products. Metallica's courtroom maneuvers demonstrate its commitment to protecting not only its work, but also its image. Copyright and trademark protections are extended every day to businesses and individuals that want to protect their identities. But recent lawsuits from Metallica and other musicians have attempted to apply intellectual property (IP) protections like copyright and trademark not only to musical materials, but also to celebrity identities and reputations. Ashley was thus able to convince hundreds of thousands of people that Metallica was at it again, despite numerous telltale signs that the story was a sham.

Cases involving unauthorized appropriation of music usually fall under the jurisdiction of copyright law. But the spurious Metallica suit was couched as trademark, not copyright, infringement. That is, Metallica purportedly claimed that its distinctive sound and artistic character were articulated through its use of E chords followed by F chords, and that Unfaith audiences might be confused into thinking they were hearing Metallica. If this had been a real lawsuit, the judge probably would have dismissed it in a preliminary hearing on the grounds that a musical composition cannot possess a trademark.[1] The fact that so many journalists reported this story without checking their facts suggests one of two things: either a breathtaking ignorance of the basics of IP law, or more probably, weariness regarding IP litigation. The media seemed ready to treat the Metallica hoax as just another lawsuit involving piracy and trademark infringement rather than an obvious satire demonstrating the ridiculous restrictions placed on musical creators. This misanalysis and others like it are doing great harm to the producers and consumers of culture—those originally intended to benefit from IP law.

Recent applications of copyright and trademark law are provoking cynicism in many people, and justifiably so. As James Boyle, Rosemary Coombe, Lawrence Lessig, Kembrew McLeod, and Siva Vaidhyanathan have argued, increasing controls over copyrights, patents, and trademarks are blocking society's access to cultural resources.[2] Transformative appropriation, the act of referring to or quoting old works in order to create a new work, has always been a key element in thriving musical cultures. Today, appropriation connotes an exclusive or unauthorized seizure of materials. But transformative appropriation has historically functioned in a spirit of sharing, friendly competition, and homage. In the past, IP law protected against outright piracy but viewed transformative appropriation as a legitimate component of music making. Content providers (who often own the copyrights to music, films, and books) have in recent years seized upon IP law as a means of charging money for things that used to be freely available. The fees associated with producing samples and cover songs, for instance, are staggering. And the threat of litigation is enough to stop many artists and musicians from borrowing altogether.

The Metallica hoax reveals a societal malaise concerning the nature and scope of IP law, and more specifically, how it can (and should) affect musical creativity. But the Metallica story is not the only recent stunt intended to highlight the absurdities of intellectual property. In the preface to *Owning Culture: Authorship, Ownership, and Intellectual Property Law*, Kembrew McLeod describes how he applied for, and eventually received, trademark protection for the phrase "freedom of expression."[3] Incredulous that the U.S. Patent and Trademark Office should take his application seriously, McLeod then initiated a hoax lawsuit against a fictitious newspaper entitled "Freedom of Expression." McLeod hired a lawyer who was not privy to the scheme and who, to McLeod's surprise, accepted the case without the slightest hesitation. Next, McLeod sent a press release to the media, and sure enough, his local paper contacted him for an interview. The farce continued as McLeod gave a deadpan account of the events leading to the lawsuit, claiming that he was deeply concerned that customers might confuse his "Freedom of Expression" trademark with other products similarly named. McLeod used this hoax to protest the schism between the original intentions of IP law (to preserve the incentives of creativity) and its contemporary applications. IP laws can and have been used to repress our free speech right, which is theoretically guaranteed under the First Amendment. Had Kembrew wanted to, he could have prevented virtually any other company from using the term "freedom of expression."

Like the Metallica hoax, McLeod's prank spotlights a general complacence and ignorance concerning IP law. This ignorance is also apparent in an urban legend about a law that permits musicians to sample from any recording as long as the borrowed portion does not exceed five or ten seconds (depending on whom you ask). No such law exists. Yet many of the musicians and music fans interviewed for this book believe that they may sample limited amounts of material without permission. This is troubling because artists who borrow under the misapprehension that they are following the rules can be leaving themselves vulnerable to legal action.

The confusion regarding IP law reached a boiling point in 2002, when the British crossover-classical artist Mike Batt released *Classical Graffiti*. This album contains a one-minute section of silence that is necessary to separate various remixes. Batt titled the track "A One Minute of Silence" and facetiously credited it to himself and to a fictitious "Cage," in honor of John Cage's famous silent piece, 4'33". Probably in an attempt to draw attention to the absurdities of intellectual property law, Batt paid royalties to the American Society of Composers, Authors, and Publishers (ASCAP), which manages Cage's catalog. Peters Edition, Cage's publisher, responded by accusing Batt of copyright infringement. Meanwhile, ASCAP forwarded Batt's royalties check to the John Cage Trust, which cashed them in acknowledgment of Batt's so-called appropriation of Cage's silence.[4]

Again, the media displayed an inability to recognize what was obviously a publicity stunt on the part of Batt. The BBC, CNN, and the New Yorker framed this conflict as a straightforward copyright lawsuit, even though Peters Edition never actually sued Batt.[5] But more importantly, for the first few weeks that the story was attracting attention, no reporters questioned the dubious premise of a copyright claim lodged against someone who composed silence. Upon resolution of the debacle, the Web site for Peters Edition posted a statement from Nicholas Riddle, managing director of the press, saying, "We believe that honor has been settled. We do feel that the concept of a silent piece—particularly as it was credited by Mr. Batt as being co-written by 'Cage'—is a valuable artistic concept in which there is a copyright."[6] Note that Peters Edition objected specifically to the association of Cage's name with Batt's silent piece because listeners might assume the two had collaborated somehow (despite the fact that Cage died in 1992). As we'll see below, customer confusion is usually a matter of trademark law, not copyright law, because copyright protects creative material while trademark protects product attributes. Yet no report or article on this conflict pointed out that the Peters objection concerned the appropriation of a composer's identity rather than of his musical material.

Hoaxes and incredible stories like these are amusing, but the realities of the music industry are no laughing matter. We should be concerned about the future of musical creativity and the *true* impact of IP laws on artistic freedom. As chapter 1 demonstrates, the most troubling result of recent applications of IP law in the United States and much of the rest of the world is the conflation of *transformative appropriation* (e.g., when a rap artist samples a song without permission) with *plagiarism* (e.g., copying a Beethoven symphony and claiming it as one's own) and *music piracy* (e.g., burning a compact disc and sharing it with thousands of other network users). For instance, in 1991, when Biz Markie and Warner Music were found guilty of copyright infringement for sampling Gilbert O'Sullivan's "Alone Again (Naturally)" without permission, these qualitative distinctions ended up dissolving in the eyes of the law. Invoking the Seventh Commandment's admonition against stealing, New York District Court judge Kevin Duffy likened sampling to theft and ridiculed the defense's argument that sampling was an established practice among rap musicians.[7] While Judge Duffy might have been correct in faulting the defendants for unauthorized appropriation, his comments condemned sampling as plagiarism on par with wholesale cribbing. Decisions like Duffy's make it nearly impossible to balance property rights with musical genres such as hip-hop that allude to preexistent materials

The distinction between piracy and transformative appropriation was lost once again amid the controversy surrounding DJ Danger Mouse's *Grey Album* (2003), a mash-up of the Beatles' *White Album* and Jay-Z's *Black Album*. EMI, the copyright holder of the Beatles' master recordings, sent cease-and-desist letters both to DJ Danger Mouse and to Internet service providers (ISPs) whose clients were trading the mash-up. The Digital Millennium Copyright Act (DMCA) of 1998 gives EMI the right to pressure ISPs, but this legislation was theoretically intended to prevent rampant music piracy, not transformative reuse of material. Some readers might feel that DJ Danger Mouse is guilty of copyright infringement; others celebrate the *Grey Album* as a revolutionary original composition. But even those who condemn Danger Mouse can probably agree that EMI's threat to sue the twenty-year-old for millions of dollars (a figure commonly seen in music piracy lawsuits) was severely disproportionate to whatever economic harm, if any, resulted from the *Grey Album*. Plus, the clause in the DMCA that empowers ISPs to cut off service to their users was initially intended to curb mass copying; singling out trafficking of the *Grey Album* seems dangerously close to censorship rather than a solution to piracy infringements.

Courtroom ideologues and corporate bullies are undermining the balance that used to exist in American IP law. The time has come to separate the truth from the misunderstandings that hinder the public's ability to make responsible decisions concerning intellectual property. This requires that we distinguish piracy and plagiarism from transformative appropriation, an activity that has characterized global musical production throughout history.

Before the twentieth century, transformative appropriation in music took the form of *allusion*. For instance, a composer could refer to the work of another by writing in a similar style, or a performer could one-up a rival by imitating his performance. Musical allusion was usually unregulated, and in many contexts it was not only tolerated but *expected* of composers. With the advent of recording and replay technologies in the early twentieth century, musicians gained the power to *duplicate* sounds literally rather than simply approximate them through allusion. Duplication muddied the previously clear distinction between transformative appropriation on the one hand, and piracy and plagiarism on the other. Without well-defined criteria for distinguishing among these, judges are left to create their own methods for determining whether a sonic collage artist is merely copying someone else or whether the resulting artwork *transforms* its constituent parts. This tension between allusion and duplication peaked with the rise of disco and hip-hop turntabling and digital sampling in the 1970s and 1980s, when many musicians challenged copyright law by creating works that reused other recordings without permission. In the late 1980s, a backlash occurred in response to court decisions defending copyright holders against infringement. As an unfortunate side effect, copyright infringement was redefined to include not only plagiarism and piracy, but also both forms of transformative appropriation: duplication *and* allusion.

With the rise of disco, hip-hop, and electronic dance music, transformative appropriation has become the most important technique of today's composers and songwriters. Yet the cost of legally licensing master recordings is prohibitive, while unauthorized appropriation carries the risk of lawsuits with heavy monetary and criminal punishment. Kembrew McLeod and Siva Vaidhyanathan have both concluded that IP law is exerting a chilling effect on musical creativity, ultimately leading to a weakening of music's ability to communicate.[8] Lawrence Lessig has argued that our present system allows only the very rich, or the very obscure, to appropriate without fear of reprisal.[9] Lessig is right in condemning the expansion of IP protections to boundaries far beyond what the original framers had in mind. But we should be careful not to think that underground culture is simply a passive victim at the hands of overzealous corporate IP police. From a policy-making perspective, Lessig, McLeod, and Vaidhyanathan are right; we should be outraged. But in reality, excessive enforcement of IP laws is (despite itself) spurring many artists to rebel by finding innovative, subversive ways of communicating through transformative appropriation.

IP laws have influenced the careers and compositional choices of many artists who either allude to or duplicate other compositions in their own works. For instance, expensive litigation has fundamentally changed Public Enemy's sound by making the group unwilling to sample music anymore. Yet independent artists like DJ Spooky avoid costly licensing by sampling obscure music or else by altering their samples beyond the point of recognition. Still others (like John Oswald and Negativland) flout the copyright regime altogether by making copyright infringement a chief concern in their work. To argue for a consistent, predictable correspondence between IP law and musical creativity, however, would be unwise, if not impossible. After all, the relationship is dynamic, and the circumstances of particular musicians can vary widely. Legal scholars have observed that the very existence of certain laws influences behavior, even though such laws may never be enforced through litigation. Before the sexual revolution of the 1960s, for example, judges in American divorce trials presided over every aspect of the split, from alimony to child support and visitation. As gender roles shifted and divorce lost some of its taboo status, family law began providing a framework in which husbands and wives could negotiate their separations outside of the courtroom. Robert H. Mnookin and Lewis Kornhauser refer to this phenomenon as the "shadow" of law exerting an indirect influence on bargaining and decision making.[10] We can understand the effects of IP law on transformative musical appropriation similarly, whereby legal restrictions and the potential for punishment influence the choices of musicians. Some artists respond to these impediments with innovative borrowing strategies and fresh materials, while others suffer from having their aesthetic possibilities reduced. Both scenarios give us ample reason to study the relationships between IP law and musical creativity. For if left unscrutinized, applications of IP law will deprive us of the sort of artistic and cultural abundance that we used to be able to take for granted.

CHAPTER ONE

Music as Intellectual Property

If you went to an American movie theater in 2003, chances are you saw one of four public service announcements produced by the organization Respect Copyrights, all of which begin with the caption, "Who makes movies?" One of these films features Manny Perry, a stuntman who describes the dangers involved in filming an action sequence. We see a car chase from the thriller *Enemy of the State*. The camera then returns to Manny's weathered but kindly face as he likens free downloading of a movie to stealing a candy bar. The screen then shows three consecutive captions: "Manny Perry makes movies," "Put an end to piracy," and "Movies. They're worth it."[1]

The Motion Picture Association of America (MPAA) devised this ad campaign to counteract the pirating of films through bootlegging and Internet file sharing. This commercial packs an emotional punch: it uses patriotic-sounding music in the style of Aaron Copland, and it co-opts a popular movie to remind us how exciting action sequences can be. But most importantly, it recasts copyright infringement, a supposedly victimless crime, as injurious to a likable, presumably working-class individual. By giving a face to film production, the Respect Copyrights campaign appeals to our sense of fairness.

What this commercial doesn't tell us, however, is that the copyrights to films are owned not by stuntmen, or by actors, or even by directors or screenwriters. Instead, film production companies

11

own them and distribute royalties among the various individuals involved in a movie's creation. The MPAA did not undertake this campaign merely to protect the grips or stuntmen who earn a day-to-day living working on films. Production companies are panicking at revenue losses that threaten the salaries of CEOs who often do not participate at all in the creative process of making movies.

The Respect Copyrights campaign is a recent example of a centuries-old strategy on the part of publishers to cast copyright as a *moral right.* According to their stance, copyright promotes creativity by ensuring that authors can control and profit from their own work. As we'll see below, this argument brushes aside the fact that most authors do not own the copyrights to their work; they sell them to a publisher or record label in exchange for a share in the royalties and a guarantee that their work will be distributed commercially. Nevertheless, the concept of copyright as a moral right rests on our belief that it's only fair to compensate authors for their work. The moral right argument advocating the existence of copyright has coexisted with and, in some cases, competed with an alternative justification concerning the benefits that copyright imparts to society as a whole. According to this other argument, copyright is desirable because it provides a short-term economic incentive (i.e., royalties) that encourages authors to create. But most changes to intellectual property law have been undertaken in the name of moral rights. From the English publishers in the seventeenth century to today's Disney executives, those seeking to amend IP law say they are supporting the rights of authors over their work. This argument has generally succeeded because it appeals to society's desire for justice. Unfortunately, the invocations of authors' rights that we come across today are misleading, if not insincere. The true beneficiaries of recent IP law changes are neither authors nor consumers, but rather corporate content providers.

America's information and entertainment industries are entrenched in a fierce debate concerning the moral rights and economic incentive justifications for copyright. These two perspectives offer radically different visions of what the parameters of copyright ought to be. Those who claim to sponsor moral rights want to extend copyright protections in terms of both scope and duration in order to ensure continued royalties. Those who advocate the economic incentive theory argue that expanding copyright durations will stunt future creativity. Content providers like the MPAA and the Recording Industry Association of America (RIAA) would have us believe that society must buttress copyright in order to prevent piracy. But the same laws that restrict a pirate's ability to bootleg DVDs and CDs are also inhibiting artists and musicians from creating new material through the transformation of preexisting works. When the United States was founded, copyright was enforced in order to discourage copying, but today it has been commandeered by the music and film industries to preempt transformative appropriation. So while ad campaigns like Respect Copyrights appear to present a reasonable argument to consumers, the implications of recent copyright-expanding legislation pose a grave threat to our ability to cultivate creativity, the very activity copyright is supposed to promote.

Since there are already several outstanding books on the history of intellectual property law, this chapter provides a selective view of key moments in the development of intellectual property. In the current war of words between the moral rights and economic incentive advocates of copyright, the casualty has been transformative appropriation, which went from coexisting peacefully with copyright laws to being regulated and even outlawed. American society is advancing toward a pay-per-use model in which consumers pay each time they want to view a film or listen to a song. While a seemingly effective method of thwarting piracy, a permissions-culture paradigm would also threaten forms of transformative appropriation that characterize some of today's most engaging music.

THE BEGINNINGS OF COPYRIGHT

The concept of "intellectual property" first took shape with the development of the printing press. Before the press, writings were copied by hand, a labor-intensive activity that ensured limited circulation for all but a few writings. Printing not only enabled rapid and practically unlimited distribution of written works, but it also introduced a new batch of questions. Who had the right to copy and sell content, the author or the publisher? And how could governments control the dissemination of seditious or undesirable writings? Copyright (literally, "the right to make copies") was invented to answer these questions. Simply put, the copyright holder controls the public life of a work. A copyright holder can choose how the work is to be published and disseminated and can charge others a fee for the right to reprint or borrow from the work. In England and France during the sixteenth century, entrepreneurs seeking to enter the printing business solicited their respective monarchs for "letters patent," or privileges granting the right to print documents such as statutes, liturgical books, and legal texts. Letters patent were effectively the first copyrights, and rulers bestowed them not on authors, but on publishers who printed materials the government approved. In England, these publishers were united in a guild called the Stationers' Company, which enjoyed a monopoly over all sanctioned printing in the British Isles until 1694, when the House of Commons voted not to extend its privileges.[2] In France, sanctioned publishers were an oligarchy of individual houses in Paris that competed against pirate presses.

Initially a tool of censorship, copyright in England matured during the 1600s into an incentive for creation and competition within the publishing industry. For the sixteenth-century English monarchy, embroiled as it was in a bloody feud over religious and temporal authority, the ability to control public opinion was of supreme importance.[3] Radical or seditious literature could further threaten the imperiled nobility. During the late seventeenth century, however, England was shifting to an increasingly representative, mercantile society whose government's stability depended on its ability to cultivate financial prosperity. By 1694 the need for exclusive copying privileges was obsolete, so Parliament eliminated the Stationers' Company's perpetual copyright. For the next sixteen years, intense competition between various English publishers led to a drop in prices for printed goods. Meanwhile, pirated copies of copyrighted works flooded the market. The Stationers' Company petitioned Parliament to restore its monopoly, but realizing that its cries were falling on deaf ears, it began to lobby for the rights of authors. Advocating authors' rights was a sly move because the publisher took for granted that upon an author's death, any copyrights belonging to the deceased would be assigned exclusively to the Stationers' Company. In 1710 Parliament responded by issuing the Statute of Anne, which assigned copyright control not to publishers, but to authors. Unlike previous publishers' monopolies, however, the Statute of Anne bestowed copyright only for a limited term of fourteen years with one possible renewal period of fourteen years. In order to encourage free trade, Parliament stipulated that the Stationers' Company could no longer enjoy a monopoly, meaning that works with expiring copyrights could not be assigned exclusively to one publisher. In effect, the Stationers' Company's lobbying backfired, dismantling the very privilege system it had hoped to reinstate.[4]

Much the same thing happened in France: as the demand for

book printing expanded in the sixteenth and seventeenth centuries, provincial presses began to threaten the dominance of the municipal houses. Fearing that the royalty might grant privileges to the country printers rather than to themselves, Parisian presses began to advocate authors' rights, just as their English counterparts had done. Authors could rarely afford to publish their own books, so they would sell copyrights to the printer who offered the most money. Since the Parisian presses had much more investment backing than most country publishers, an author-assigned copyright system would provide them in the long run with more control over the publishing industry. The conflict between provincial and city publishers raged in France until 1777, when Louis XVI decreed that authors could receive copyright privileges of indefinite duration. Once that privilege had been transferred to a printer, however, it lasted only until the author's death. The decree broke up the monopoly of municipal printers by allowing authors the final say in where their works would be printed. But after the 1789 revolution, most royal privileges were abolished. In 1793 the French parliament adopted a law that gave authors (or their appointed successors) exclusive reproduction rights that lasted for the life of the author plus ten years. This law proved to be one of the most influential in copyright history, informing German and Swiss copyright regimes as well as those of most civil law countries.[5]

There are two important lessons to draw from this preliminary history. First, most changes to copyright, from the seventeenth century to the present day, have been undertaken in the name of authors. When English and French publishers petitioned their governments to reinstate perpetual copyrights, they did so while purporting to champion authors' interests. The idea that an author could possess rights over his writings had been circulating in European intellectual circles during the late seventeenth century, in part due to John

Locke's theory of "natural rights," which he expounded in his *Second Treatise of Civil Government* of 1690. According to Locke, each person, regardless of social class, has certain inherent, or natural, rights. Locke argued that two fundamental natural rights were control over one's own body and control over the fruits of one's labor; for Locke, labor was the "unquestionable property of the laborer."[6] The tendency of publishers to invoke authors persists to this day—just recall the MPAA's "Respect Copyright" publicity campaign.

Second, the moral rights and economic incentive models differ in terms of the centrality of the author in determining the scope and function of copyright. After its 1789 revolution, France instituted a copyright regime that was based *prima facie* on authors' rights, as evidenced by the fact that the copyright duration lasted the duration of an author's life plus ten years. On the other hand, England's 1710 Statute of Anne advocated the economic incentive philosophy by placing definitive limits on copyright periods, irrespective of the author's lifespan, and by making works with lapsed copyrights available for anyone to reprint and distribute. The Statute of Anne gave independent publishers a reason to enter the business, but the ultimate beneficiaries of the law were consumers, who enjoyed lower prices as a result of competition.

The U.S. Constitution granted Congress the right to legislate a federal copyright law (as well as a patent law pertaining to inventions) that applied to all states uniformly. The fledgling nation naturally drew inspiration from the economic incentive paradigm of its former ruler, Britain:

> The Congress shall have the power to [. . .] promote the progress of science and useful arts, by securing for limited times to authors and inventors the exclusive rights to their respective writings and discoveries [.][7]

In 1790 Congress issued the first Copyright Act, which, like the
Statute of Anne, specified a fourteen-year term with one possible
renewal of fourteen years. Copyright protection was available only to
book, map, or chart authors who registered their works in compliance
with the law. In the words of its framers, the Act was intended "to
encourage learning."[8]

MUSIC COPYRIGHT IN THE UNITED STATES, 1790–1909

Consider "The Star Spangled Banner." You can own a copy of its
sheet music, sing it at the opening of a local baseball game, and
listen to Jimi Hendrix's famous Woodstock performance. You can
physically hold a recording of Hendrix's rendition if you find it in
a used record shop, and you can also download this same recording
as intangible, digital data through a file-sharing service like Kazaa
or Morpheus. All these permutations qualify as "The Star Spangled
Banner" but possess different commercial and legal statuses. There
is no single definitive form of a piece of music in the way that there
is one first edition of A *Tale of Two Cities* from which subsequent
editions have been copied.

This ontological multiplicity has rendered the incorporation of
music into intellectual property regimes challenging at best. England, France, and the United States developed copyright laws concerned primarily with printed texts and images, laws that were
retroactively (and often clumsily) applied to music. For instance,
the States' 1790 Act protected books, charts, and maps, but the
term "book" was interpreted broadly to include virtually all printed
media, including sheet music.[9] As music publishing became a competitive industry in the 1820s, publishers complained that composers were being exploited. Congress amended the Copyright Act

in 1831 to include printed musical compositions under separate statutory protection.[10] The 1831 act also increased term protection to twenty-eight years with a renewal period of fourteen years. But even after 1831, music and copyright were poorly matched because copyright was intended for printed media, while music had a dual existence as sheet music and live performance. Subsequent legislation attempted to address this tension by extending coverage to other manifestations of performed music. The Dramatic Compositions Copyright Act of 1856 stated that accompanimental music for dramatic stage works enjoyed a right of public performance, meaning that a copyrighted piece could not be performed in public without the permission of its copyright holder.[11] A later amendment in 1897 granted copyright holders of all types of musical works (not just accompaniment to dramatic works) the exclusive right to perform their pieces publicly.[12] This amendment required that venue owners pay publishers and composers for the right to host performances of their works. The 1897 law was nearly impossible to enforce given that public performances can occur in so many different types of venues, from concert halls to bars to public parks. Music publishers themselves were initially hesitant to enforce payment of royalties because they regarded performances as advertisements encouraging the purchase of sheet music (at the time, their greatest source of income).[13]

Disregard for the performance right vanished as American publishers heard how their European counterparts were profiting from similar legislation. But even after opinions had shifted, the law was difficult to implement: bar owners and restaurateurs claimed not to charge their clients for any music performed in their establishments and so resisted paying licensing fees for protected songs. The American Society of Composers, Authors, and Publishers (ASCAP) and subsequent groups such as Broadcast Music Incorporated (BMI) and SESAC (formerly the Society of European Stage Authors and Composers) were created to enforce the performance right by collecting royalties for the public performance (and later, broadcast) of copyrighted works.[14] But the U.S. performance right guarantees royalties only for the copyright holder of a work, who is usually the publisher, not the songwriter. The law does not stipulate royalties for the performers who play the work, nor for the copyright holder of the sound recording. Performers' royalties can be guaranteed within an individual contract but are not legislated.

By the early twentieth century, the development of player pianos enabled even wider dissemination of musical content. These automated musical instruments could read information inscribed as holes on a long stream of paper, known as a piano roll. The piano roll was the ancestor of the vinyl record and compact disc: the first medium to permit "mechanical reproduction" (i.e., replay) of a composition. When piano rolls were invented, no law protected authors from having their works performed by mechanical means because the 1897 performance right act applied only to live performances by humans, not mechanized replay. Congress issued a new copyright act in 1909 to address this omission. The 1909 Act maintained the copyright protection term at twenty-eight years but increased the renewal term to twenty-eight years from fourteen years. This act also introduced a new "right of mechanical reproduction," which stipulated that once a copyrighted musical composition had been released to the public, any other recording artist could record his own version of the piece as long as he paid a licensing fee. The 1909 Act ensured that copyright holders were paid for recordings of their work as well as reprints and live performances. It also legislated out of existence exclusive contracts between piano roll companies and music publishers. Thereafter, anyone could release a piano roll

version of a distributed composition provided they reimbursed the
copyright holder with a statutory royalty, the so-called compulsory
license fee.

MUSIC AND U.S. IP LAW IN THE TWENTIETH CENTURY

There have been several formidable changes to copyright law since
1909, many of which occurred under the Copyright Act of 1976,
an overhaul of the 1909 Act. The chart on page 22 summarizes the
status of music under today's copyright laws.

The lifespan of the copyright for a composition depends on when
the piece was created and/or published. For all works created on or
after January 1, 1978, protection begins at the moment the work is
fixed onto a tangible medium of expression and lasts for the life of
the author plus 70 years. If the work is anonymous, a work for hire
(meaning a multiauthor work owned by an organization or company)[15], or of corporate authorship, the term lasts 95 years from its
time of publication, or 120 years from its time of creation, whichever
is less. For works published between the beginning of 1964 and the
end of 1977, protection begins at the moment of publication (as
long as there is a copyright notice) and lasts 28 years for its first
term. An automatic extension term of 67 years is also provided. For
works published between 1923 and the end of 1963, there is a 28-year
term beginning at the moment of publication, with an optional renewal term of 67 years.[16] As for sound recordings, only those created
on or after February 15, 1972, receive federal copyright protection.
Certain state laws protect recordings created prior to this date, but
these laws vary.

Before the 1900s, intellectual property laws were more or less
in harmony with the reproduction technologies available at the
time. But with the advent of sound recording devices, copiers, and

TABLE 1. MUSIC'S COPYRIGHT STATUS

Type of Musical Entity	Legal Definition	Who Owns the Copyright?	Scope of Protection
Compositions	An original work consisting of musical material (some combination of melody, harmony, and rhythm). Lyrics to nondramatic musical works are included in the composition copyright.	The author if s/he is self-published. Most publishing contracts require composers and songwriters to transfer copyrights.	Protects against unauthorized copying, distribution, derivative works, and performance. Mechanical reproductions of compositions are covered under a compulsory license, meaning that anyone can re-record a published composition as long as they give written notice to the Copyright Office and pay the statutory royalty rate on each record made and distributed.
Sound Recordings	Any work in which musical, spoken, or other sounds are fixated onto any medium (excluding sounds accompanying films).	Most record companies require control of a sound recording copyright as a condition for album release. The owner of a recording may or may not be the owner for the composition it contains.	Protects against unauthorized copying and distribution. Reuse of a recording is not covered under a compulsory license, meaning that licensing must be negotiated before the recording is appropriated into a new work.

computers, reproduction has become accessible to a large segment of the population within a short period of time. For much of the twentieth century, American intellectual property laws lagged several decades behind the latest reproduction technologies. For instance, media containing data for mechanical reproduction, whether wax cylinders, piano rolls, records, or cassette tapes, were not covered under federal copyright until the 1970s, despite the economic value of jazz, pop, rock 'n' roll, and rock recordings. Not until the passing of the Sound Recording Act of 1971 was federal protection extended to all sound recordings fixed and published on or after February 15, 1972, regardless of the type of media on which they were fixed.[17] Like the 1909 Act, the Sound Recording Act was a belated effort to keep abreast of technological innovation. After all, the invention of playback technology, whether piano roll or vinyl record, was as revolutionary as the printing press because it permitted distribution of sounds to large audiences.

Although the Sound Recording Act arrived several decades late, it at least offered a form of protection suited to evolving technology. Unfortunately, most other recent modifications to IP law are ideally calibrated to reproduction technologies of the nineteenth century, when copying was slower and costlier. These modifications assume that if IP law worked during the nineteenth century, then more of the same IP law will work even better in the twentieth and twenty-first centuries. The majority of changes to the copyright regime, for instance, have expanded either the lifespan or the scope of protection; these amendments fail to acknowledge new modes of cultural production, from postmodern novels to hip-hop, that challenge our definitions of borrowing and infringement. The copyright duration for a musical composition has increased from its original duration of fourteen years to its current limit of the composer's life plus seventy years. The scope of copyright has ballooned to include uses of content that were previously unregulated. Lawrence Lessig points out that in 1790, transformative appropriation of American copyrighted materials was entirely legal and required no licensing, whereas transformation today is usually permitted only when appropriators pay licensing fees. Unauthorized transformation is prosecuted with the same laws and penalties that address piracy.[18]

During its first 150 years of existence, the United States distinguished itself for having laws expressly written to incentivize the creativity of its own citizens. While copyrights and trademarks did exist, their limited scope and duration allowed appropriation and transformation, which is the type of "piracy" that Lawrence Lessig and Siva Vaidhyanathan describe as central to works by Walt Disney and the Marx Brothers.[19] Indeed, until recently, the United States was the most infamous "pirate nation" in the world because it protected its own copyrights while offering scant protection, if any, to foreign copyrighted works.[20] If we could fault America's nascent IP laws for anything, it would be for not respecting copyright *enough.* Yet today, American IP laws protect the interests of content owners while making creative work involving transformation costlier and more difficult. Two factors explain this philosophical shift.

First, the dominance of the United States over digital technology industries has been a mixed blessing. This leadership position has obviously yielded significant economic rewards, but it has also made the United States vulnerable to piracy of creative content by means of the very tools it pioneered: computers. While during the nineteenth and early twentieth centuries the United States was the site for pirating of foreign books, maps, and paintings, America's cash cows of today—software, recorded music, and film—are being illegally traded throughout the world. The United States has tried to shore up international support for the integrity of its copyrights by calibrating its own laws with those of its allies and by joining

multilateral IP law treaties such as the Berne Convention and the
World Intellectual Property Organization (WIPO).[21] An underpin-
ning of the Berne Convention is the idea that an author should
control not only the reproduction of the work, but also the circumstances under which a work is used and appropriated. The WIPO
allows performers to prevent parodies of their work from being made.
Entertainment and information corporations like Disney and Time
Warner endorsed synchronization with Berne and WIPO because
shifting to a moral-rights-based paradigm actually increases control
over content and allows content providers to charge fees for acts of
transformative appropriation that used to be free.

Second, content providers and artists' representatives are attempt-
ing to close the loopholes in music copyright by employing parallel
IP law regimes. For instance, the right of publicity (once reserved for
the families of dead entertainers) and trademark law (which used
to apply only to logos and slogans) are now empowering celebrity
singers to prevent impersonations of their vocal performance styles
(see chapter 2). Trademark and the right of publicity are entirely
separate from copyright law and allow content providers to place
both creative and economic values on performance style and timbre,
attributes that used to be part of the public domain.

Given the increasing protection terms for copyright and the expansion of non-copyright regimes, one might naturally wonder whether
borrowing and transformative appropriation are even legal under
U.S. law. These activities were, in fact, guaranteed protection under
the fair use provision of the Copyright Act of 1976, which allows
appropriation of protected works under limited circumstances. Portions of copyrighted material may be borrowed and incorporated in
a new work, provided that it is used "for purposes such as criticism,
comment, news reporting, teaching (including multiple copies for
classroom use), scholarship, or research."[22] The law requires that

four factors be considered when deciding whether a borrowing qualifies as fair use:

> 1) the purpose and character of the use, including whether such use
> is of a commercial nature or is for nonprofit educational purposes;
>
> 2) the nature of the copyrighted work;
>
> 3) the amount and substantiality of the portion used in relation to
> the copyrighted work as a whole; and
>
> 4) the effect of the use upon the potential market for or value of the
> copyrighted work.

The Copyright Act instructs courts to balance these four factors,
since different types of appropriation spring from different artistic
intentions and affect their source materials differently. Legislators
defined fair use vaguely in order to avoid a compulsory licensing
scenario where certain types of appropriation would always be per-
missible while others would always be illegal.

The fair use provision should, in theory, justify many types of musical appropriation, especially those that contain criticism or parody
and those that borrow relatively small amounts of material. Yet most
managers and entertainment lawyers discourage their clients from
relying on fair use as a means of bypassing the licensing process (see
chapter 4). In an ideal world, artists and copyright holders would
agree in advance on which types of appropriation count as fair use.
But fair use is a defense, invoked only after a copyright holder files
an infringement lawsuit. Musicians who sample and appropriate are
often loath to defend themselves in court because of the cost of
mounting a defense. And despite the most famous case involving
music and fair use, *Acuff-Rose v. Campbell* (involving 2 Live Crew's
borrowing of Roy Orbison's "Oh, Pretty Woman"), there is a paucity
of case law describing which types of musical appropriation qualify
as fair use.

THE CASE FOR TRANSFORMATIVE APPROPRIATION

Whatever the current viability of the fair use provision, its very existence tells us that the framers of the 1976 Copyright Act saw fit to legitimize transformative appropriation. Efforts by content providers to curtail the fair use privilege are new in the history of intellectual property. In earlier decades and centuries, neither legislators nor publishers paid much attention to small-scale borrowing and appropriation, which occurred largely unimpeded. Why did no one seem bothered by transformative appropriation in the past, and why is it suddenly so threatening?

By definition, transformative appropriation implies creators' engagement with and reaction to other creators' works. Yet at various points during the twentieth century, transformative appropriation was challenged by a new concept of creativity valorizing authors who claimed not to borrow from their surroundings or fellow artists. The tendency to view creative activities as private, atomized pursuits was implicitly encouraged by copyright laws that, after all, were designed to protect works having one identifiable author. As Michel Foucault explains, the construct of the author as an isolated genius also gained currency because books and compositions with one author seem more prestigious than those with several, or those whose authorship is unknown.[23] Modernists in the Western art music and jazz camps vigorously argued that true genius entailed originality and complete independence from tradition. Arnold Schoenberg, who developed atonal and twelve-tone music in the early twentieth century, critiqued his peers' practice of quoting folk music in their compositions. He claimed:

A composer—a real composer—composes only if he has something to say which has not yet been said and which he feels must be said: a

musical message to music lovers. Under what circumstances can he
feel the urge to write something that has already been said, as it has in
the case of the static treatment of folk songs?[24]

Similarly, the jazz percussionist Mtume, who played with Miles
Davis in the 1970s, condemned transformative appropriation in
hip-hop as "artistic necrophilia," asserting that musicians must constantly develop new modes of communication.[25]

The ideal of the author as a lone genius contradicts the fact that
transformative appropriation has informed most musical traditions.
The communal aspects of folk, African, and African American musical cultures are widely acknowledged.[26] As Henry Louis Gates has
demonstrated, much of the creative culture of the African Diaspora
participates in a process he calls *signifyin'*, in which a new work comments on past works through parody, mockery, or praise.[27] Perhaps
less obvious is the fact that classical music (i.e., European concert
repertoire from the eighteenth and nineteenth centuries) also ex-
hibited a vibrant culture of transformative appropriation rather than
isolated inspiration. In 1822 the British music critic F. W. Horncastle wrote, "in these enlightened days, when art seems to have
reached its very utmost perfection, and science its most refined fin-
ish, there must be a considerable portion of unconscious imitation
in almost all their productions."[28] Horncastle by no means advocated plagiarism or lazy derivation; in the same article, he wrote,
"Originality in any art or science is considered by the critics a most
essential quality in the works of either the theorist or practitioner
who puts forward any claim to public notice."[29] For Horncastle, truly
original composers were able to integrate influences of musicians
they admired with their own authorial voices. Other musicologists
were even more permissive of borrowing. Constantin von Sternberg

argued in 1919 that reshaping previously composed material was a legitimate, standard practice among esteemed composers like Frédéric Chopin, Josef Haydn, and Wolfgang Amadeus Mozart. Plagiarism occurred not when a composer borrowed someone else's ideas, but rather when he added nothing new to them.[30] Hugh Arthur Scott asserted in 1927 that some very common musical elements (like scales or cadences) must be considered as public property, not the personal signatures of individual composers.[31]

When we disengage from modernist prejudices against transformative appropriation, we can observe that in jazz, folk, and Western art music, there is an ethical and legal continuum connecting the extremes of excessive derivativeness and utter originality, a continuum Paul Geller refers to as the "spectrum from copying to creation."[32] Until the twentieth century, three types of activities inhabited this spectrum: piracy, plagiarism, and allusion. Piracy, the mass reproduction of whole works, was generally viewed as ethically and legally wrong. Plagiarism, an author's false claim of another's work, was also deemed illegal and unethical. Yet allusion, the incorporation of aspects of others' style or work into one's own, was an ethical gray zone, sometimes hailed as skillful genius and at other times discounted as lack of inspiration. To claim that a work displayed no traces of allusion, however, was untenable. The very act of composition necessitated a reaction to preexisting music.

The fundamental change wrought by sound reproduction technologies of the twentieth century has been to enlarge the gray zone between plagiarism and allusion by introducing another category of imitation: mechanical reproduction. In other words, by 1990, digital technologies enabled a fourth activity on the spectrum from copying to creation, which now includes piracy, plagiarism, *duplication*, and allusion. Reproduction technologies such as sound recording devices and digital samplers enable piracy on a mass scale, as well as selective copying that could allow musicians to plagiarize. These technologies also allow musicians to create imaginative, original collages of preexisting music. Unfortunately, U.S. IP law, which has not yet come to terms with these distinctions, summarily prosecutes all acts of duplication in the same way, as if they all constituted piracy.

CHAPTER TWO

Arrangements and Musical Allusion

The voice of Elvis Presley is perhaps the most contested acoustic phenomenon in modern culture. Despite abundant proof that Elvis happened onto rock 'n' roll well after its inception, popular histories still credit him with single-handedly inventing rock 'n' roll and popularizing it with white audiences who may never have had contact with black music. For legions of fans, Elvis's voice brought about a cultural and musical revolution, breaking down racial and sexual barriers and inciting adolescents to rebel against their elders. Yet to his detractors, who accuse him of passing off black musical forms as his own, Elvis's voice was an instrument of artistic theft. The poet Gil Scott-Heron bitterly claimed that Elvis was "no new thing" because he fit into a long tradition of white co-optation of black cultural identity. For Scott-Heron, Presley and his successors in blue-eyed soul and white funk proved that blacks were still being victimized by cultural appropriation, making their contributions to American history virtually invisible and inaudible.

The King is dead, but his corpse and voice remain subjects of controversy. Elvis Presley Enterprises, Inc. (EPE), is the legal guardian of his image and in recent years has succeeded in outlawing the production of kitschy "Elvis on black velvet" paintings. EPE polices television shows and films to ensure that all invocations of Elvis are "pre-cleared," meaning that appropriators have applied for permission and paid for the right to use Elvis's image.[1] In Las Vegas, Elvis Presley impersonators are as common as slot machines, but EPE has sued the more successful ones in an attempt to regulate public uses of his persona.[2] The control over Elvis's public image extends over not only his physical appearance and stage mannerisms but also the very quality of his voice. Impersonators who want to exhibit their vocal resemblance to Elvis can legally do so only after paying EPE.

To begin with Elvis Presley's voice is fitting because it resonates at the heart of debates concerning the ethics and legality of musical allusion. Content providers such as Time Warner, Disney, and EPE are anxious to control all aspects of celebrity identity, particularly acoustic traits. In essence, these efforts are intended to reclassify previously unprotected qualities such as voice and performance style as intellectual property. Copyright protection for music is more porous than protections afforded to other creative works, and until a few decades ago allowed for relatively unencumbered imitation and impersonation. The melody and lyrics of a copyrighted composition enjoy unambiguous protection, but generally such coverage does not also include stylistic elements such as form or instrumentation. The rationale behind such a split is that melody and lyrics are the expressive heart of a piece, while nuances such as timbre, ornamentation, and instrumentation add to, but do not fundamentally change, the expressive impact of a work.

Expression is indeed at the heart of this discussion. American copyright purports to protect expressions of ideas, but not the ideas themselves. With novels and buildings, it is relatively easy to point to the definitive expression or product resulting from an initial idea. Yet music resists classification as an idea or expression because there is so little agreement as to the precise nature of music (a concept referred to in metaphysics as its *ontology*). When does music cease to be an idea and start to become an expression? Some might answer, "When it is performed." But if this were true, copyright would not exist for sheet music, only for performances and recordings. To pose a more fundamental question, how exactly do we define music in the first place?

In Western theory, music comprises melody, harmony, rhythm, and formal structure. Yet this narrow description ignores style, stage presence, and the timbre of particular instruments. The definition of music has changed significantly in the past two decades, reflecting a shift in the core values of the international music industry. Adding to the elusiveness of a definition is the fact that music is not a widely "read" or "understood" language in the way that printed or spoken languages are. Whereas the origins of printed phrases are usually unambiguous (e.g., one can prove that the passage "It was the best of times, it was the worst of times" was first penned by Charles Dickens), the origins of a musical idea are open to speculation. The beginning of Cream's "White Room" (1968) contains chords that bear more than a passing resemblance to the opening of the famous aria "Visi d'Arte" from Giocomo Puccini's opera *Tosca* (1900). But it is unclear whether the members of Cream were even aware of the connection to Puccini; the similarities could be a matter of musical coincidence. Without recourse to interviews, we would never know for sure if the passage were an ironic reference, plagiarism, or innocent serendipity.

The perplexity concerning music's ontology is traceable to shifts within the past two hundred years in the status of printed notation. Before the Romantic era (roughly 1800–1900), scores, printed music, and manuscripts were performance aids but were rarely viewed as definitive sources of music in and of themselves.[3] But by the beginning of the nineteenth century, the role of sheet music had evolved from being a mere guideline to being the sole authoritative version

of a piece. Ludwig van Beethoven, Richard Wagner, and Johannes
Brahms, vanguards of German Romantic composition, wrote pieces
whose fundamental incarnations were the scores themselves. Performances were merely imperfect manifestations of the notated ideas.
The private correspondence of these composers mentions mutinous
prima donnas and inept instrumentalists who marred their pieces
beyond recognition. The resulting frustration of these composers
underscores the fact that they considered sheet music the primary
source of musical content. Recordings, of course, did not exist at
this time, and live performances were too ephemeral to have any
long-term significance. Virtuosi like Franz Liszt or Niccolò Paganini
admittedly captured the imaginations of audiences, but their noto-
riety ultimately succeeded in generating the sale of sheet music.

Vaudeville and Tin Pan Alley music publishers at the end of the
nineteenth century and start of the twentieth were usually European musicians whose businesses depended on healthy sheet music
sales.[4] But these publishers also relied on live performances and early
recording technologies such as piano rolls, both as separate sources of
income and as means of increasing the demand for printed music.
Copyright law changed to accommodate the shift towards profit-
generating performances. As mentioned previously, the Dramatic
Compositions Copyright Act of 1856 and the Copyright Amendment Act of 1897 were the first laws to protect performances of
copyrighted compositions, yet these laws still gave priority to written
forms. In other words, only after proving ownership of a written work
could a copyright holder license the right to perform it publicly. The
1909 Copyright Act instituted compulsory licensing for mechanical
reproductions, meaning that publishers were guaranteed royalties
when their works were recorded. But sound recordings themselves
were not included under statutory copyright protection until 1971
with the passing of the Sound Recording Act, which instituted a

separate copyright for sound recordings independent of the copyright for the underlying composition. Well before the 1971 Act, however, recordings began to eclipse both sheet music and live performances and became the dominant medium for musical distribution. This trend became evident during the 1940s and 1950s, when musicians' unions in the United States and Great Britain fought a losing battle to block the replay of recordings at parties and social occasions, events that had previously showcased live music.[5] The increase of popular music's (and particularly rock 'n' roll's) market share meant that listeners consumed music more often through home listening than through concert attendance or home performance.[6] In other words, music consumption has metamorphosed in the past century from an active occupation in which consumers buy printed pieces in order to play music on their own to a passive occupation in which consumers buy recorded pieces and simply listen to them. Contemporary musical habits are vastly different from those of one hundred years ago due to the proliferation of consumer recordings and radio, television, and Internet broadcasting. Recordings are so much a fixture of the popular music experience that Theodore Gracyk has proposed a rock aesthetics centering on the recording rather than live performance or sheet music.[7] This recording-based perspective challenges the score-centered foundations of Romantic composition, because for one particular "piece," there can exist many different versions, covers, arrangements, or remixes, each of them protectable and none more primary or more significant than the next. If by the beginning of the twenty-first century the recording is the primary source of content, then what does this suggest about music today? Does a musical composition *really* exist in printed form? As an arrangement? As a recording?

To answer these questions, consider when copyright goes into effect. The 1976 Copyright Act stipulates that protection for a new work begins the moment it is fixed onto any tangible medium. This rule differs from the previous 1909 Copyright Act, which required that a composition be fixed onto paper and distributed publicly before expressions (recordings, performances) could be protected. With the 1976 Act, fixation can be simultaneous with transmission, excluding "purely evanescent or transient reproductions such as those projected briefly on a screen, shown electronically on a television or other cathode ray tube, or captured momentarily in the 'memory' of a computer."[8] The 1976 Act undermines the authority of the "ink-and-paper" composition by protecting musical works from the moment they are fixed to any medium, whether magnetic tape, vinyl, or compact disc. So, under current legislation, sheet music is both a tangible medium and an aid to performance, a set of suggestions for how to perform or record a piece.

The implications of the 1976 Act are far-reaching, because this law produces the unintended result that *the ink-and-paper composition is now viewed less as an expression and more as an idea.* For example, publishers who release a sheet music version of a song can prevent others only from imitating its melody and lyrics. Every other musical aspect specified in the piece can be copied by someone else, meaning that things like dynamics, timbre, articulation, and rhythm bear the legal status of ideas rather than expressions. Publishers can, however, exert more comprehensive control over the actual dissemination of their work. Unauthorized photocopies of the sheet music for a piece would be illegal, as would unlicensed copies of recordings of the piece. Unlike ink-and-paper compositions, sound recordings are treated as expressions or manifestations of a compositional idea, and thus *every sound that appears on a recording is protected*; this includes not only melody and lyrics, but also harmonies, rhythms, and any other sounds that are demonstrably drawn from a preexisting recording. This distinction between sheet music as idea and performance as expression is most relevant in today's environment in which jazz and popular music showcase improvisation. In this milieu, the "composition" is protean, shifting from paper to tape to extemporization, and the premise that a piece can be captured with ink and paper has been rendered obsolete.[9]

THE DEVELOPMENT OF THE COVER LICENSE

The right to own property in the United States and several other countries entails another right: to decide when and how to part with that property. No one can force you to sell your car, even if someone offers you its full price or an amount exceeding its value. Likewise, someone who steals your car cannot expiate the crime simply by reimbursing you for the loss; the thief will still face criminal charges. Copyright is a means of controlling and protecting intellectual property, so under most circumstances, the copyright holder has complete discretion over whether to license a borrowing and how much to charge for the appropriation. But music copyright is anomalous because of the existence of the compulsory mechanical license. Anyone wanting to make a film based on an Anne Rice novel would need to seek the permission of the copyright holder, who in this case is Anne Rice herself. But anyone who abides by the conditions set forth in the Copyright Act (usually requiring a statutory licensing fee and registration) can record an arrangement of a musical work so long as it has already been recorded and released to the public. This provision allows for "cover versions": recordings of songs made by musicians other than those responsible for the original recording.

The "cover license" was adopted in the 1909 Copyright Act to address music publishers' new habit of disseminating their songs as arrangements for player pianos. The Supreme Court had ruled in the 1908 *White-Smith Music Publishing v. Apollo* decision that according to the laws then in place, mechanical recordings of copyrighted music were not derivative works and thus did not infringe on the copyrights of compositions.[10] The Court concluded that if mechanical performances were indeed felt to be copies or derivative works, then it was the responsibility of Congress to revise the copyright code to make this view explicit. Congress rose to the challenge with its 1909 revision to the Copyright Act, requiring that mechanically produced performances be subject to approval by the copyright holder in order to ensure that artists and publishers receive royalties. But the 1909 Act also made this mechanical license compulsory by imposing a mandatory two-cent royalty payable to publishers for the recording of any copyrighted work. The compulsory license was approved to placate competitors of the Aeolian Company, a piano roll manufacturer that enjoyed an exclusive contract with the Music Publishers Association to produce player piano versions of hit songs.[11]

Piano rolls, an early form of recording merchandise, allowed customers who liked what they heard in live performances to "bring the music home" for their player pianos. But most piano roll recordings were not verbatim transcriptions of original pieces; they were arrangements, in which some element (e.g., structure, instrumentation, melody, harmony, or length) had been altered. In IP parlance, arrangements are "derivative works," spin-offs of the primary source of content, the sheet music composition. In the early years of the twentieth century, the music industry felt that mechanical reproduction was important but was not its most valuable market. Sheet music sales were still the lifeblood of the industry, tripling in wholesale value between 1890 and 1909. Yet by the 1930s and 1940s, publishers railed against the mechanical license, realizing too late that statutorily enforced licenses barred them from haggling for royalties.[12] The rise of rock 'n' roll covers in the mid-1950s was abetted by their relative affordability and ease of clearance, and consequently, recording sales utterly eclipsed those of sheet music.

The compulsory license entails "the privilege of making a musical arrangement of the work to the extent necessary to conform it to the style or manner of interpretation of the performance involved."[13] An arrangement of a musical composition is considered an alternative version of the work. It may differ from the original by being orchestrated for different instruments, or material may have been added to it, or removed. According to the Copyright Act, the copyright holder has the exclusive right "to prepare derivative works based upon the copyright work."[14] A derivative work is "based on one or more pre-existing works, such as a translation, musical arrangement, dramatization, fictionalization, motion picture version, sound recording, art reproduction, abridgement, condensation, or any other form in which a work may be recast, transformed, or adapted."[15] This means that anyone wishing to publish an arrangement would be required to seek the permission of the original copyright holder and then agree on a fee for licensing the material. In addition, the arranger would need to credit the original and could seek copyright protection only for the bits the arranger contributed to the arrangement.

The compulsory license for mechanical reproduction, however, allows the arranger to bypass the original copyright holder altogether. But in order for the compulsory license to operate, the original composition must first be distributed to the public in the form of a recording. This is hardly anomalous considering how much of today's music is recorded. For example, let's say that Eminem wants to record a version of the Beach Boys' "God Only Knows." Eminem would not need to convince the song's publishers that he should receive permission, because mechanical reproduction licensing is compulsory so long as he registers the recording as an arrangement of the original copyright holder's work and pays the statutory royalty. But Eminem would not be able to claim a copyright for his arrangement of "God Only Knows" without having reached an agreement with the publishers indicating that his recorded version adds significantly to the original.

Remarkably, the compulsory license for music allows for both considerable similarities and considerable differences between an original and a recorded arrangement. So long as he did not change the melody or the "fundamental character of the work," Eminem's version of "God Only Knows" would be recordable, even if it may not qualify for a copyright as an arrangement. Courts have traditionally interpreted this clause liberally to allow for substantial disparities between an original and its arrangements. This tolerance has enabled the production of cover versions. In R&B, soul, rock 'n' roll, and folk, cover recordings have been crucibles for experimentation such that many cover songs bear no more than a passing resemblance to their originals. On the other hand, the compulsory license also allows for the creation of sound-alikes because copyright holders of recordings cannot legally prevent others from alluding to their sounds.[16]

Theoretically speaking, recordings are expressions of musical ideas and as such can be imitated through sound-alike recordings or copied with recording and mixing technology. Yet the difference between imitation and copying is murky, given the capabilities of software such as Pro Tools that are designed to make and alter recordings. But for now, consider that when sound recordings were first granted statutory protection in the United States in 1971, analog recording technologies were primitive compared to those of today. The distinction between a copy and an imitation of a recording was relatively clear. Copying involved replaying an extant recording from magnetic tape or a vinyl disc, while imitation involved reperforming an *idea*. The structure of copyright law (and until the 1980s, the relative absence of protection for performance style and voice) meant that there were effectively two modes of transformative appropriation: allusion and duplication. According to Theodore Gracyk, allusion implies paraphrasing while duplication involves direct quotation.[17] Allusion occurs when any musician refers to another work, knowingly or otherwise. This includes arrangements, sound-alike recordings, and cover songs. Sound, however, can be mechanically *duplicated* in only one way, by playing it back after it has already been fixed onto a recording medium (DAT, vinyl, hard disk, etc.). Or as Jane Gaines has put it, allusion involves one *person* creating music in the manner of another, while duplication involves one *machine* playing music that another has recorded.[18] While Eminem might be able to sing an approximate version of "God Only Knows" in his shower with reasonable success, he has only to play "God Only Knows" on a stereo system to duplicate the Beach Boys song.

CLASSICAL, CLASSICAL-TO-POP, AND POP-TO-CLASSICAL ARRANGEMENTS

A musical allusion is a filtered version of an original work; certain elements are discarded or changed while others are retained. The development of radio and recording technologies in the twentieth century contributed to a rise in demand for a particular type of musical allusion, arrangements. Because of arrangements, works meant for highbrow concert hall attendees have made it into animated films; works intended as love ballads have become the stuff of jazz jam sessions; works written by and for blacks have been accepted as standard white-radio fare.

Arrangements are the oldest and most common form of musical allusion. At one extreme, arranging can entail strict adaptation of a preexisting composition to a new instrumentation (for example, adapting a symphony movement for wind quintet). At the other, arranging implies substantial departures from the original work (for example, using the melody of an opera aria to construct an instrumental fantasy). Arrangements have existed in the West at least as far back as the first inclusion of Christian plainchant into early polyphony, so they are easy to take for granted as a natural part of the musical landscape. Yet the popularity of arrangements of early-nineteenth-century music compelled Congress to formalize copyright for compositions in 1831, the first moment in history when arrangements were subject to regulation.[19]

Nineteenth-century arrangements enabled soloists and chamber musicians to perform works originally written for larger forces such as symphonies or full opera companies.[20] Franz Liszt, one of the most successful traveling pianists of the era, established himself through transcriptions of arias, symphonies, and even other piano pieces. Some arrangements were deliberately simplified to encourage their sale among amateur musicians (for example, Liszt's straightforward arrangement of the Prelude to Act I of Richard Wagner's *Tristan und Isolde*). Others were extremely virtuosic, allowing Liszt to showcase his stupefying performing abilities. The popularity of arrangements in nineteenth-century concert music may seem counterintuitive given the growing belief in the sanctity and inviolability of the composition. In fact, many composers arranged their own works in order to preempt others from doing so, as Beethoven did with the piano concerto version of his Violin Concerto or Brahms did with transcriptions of his Piano Trio. These arrangements were concessions to the prevailing demand for playable home versions for various instruments, but the fact that Beethoven and Brahms were themselves the arrangers also suggests a desire to release a definitive arrangement (an oxymoron!) before someone else beat them to it. At their best, arrangements could be faithful adaptations; at their worst, they could appear to trivialize their original source material. By the mid–twentieth century, the popularity of classical music arrangements intended for concert hall performance tapered off largely because radio broadcast and recordings replaced the piano as the preferred tools of home musical entertainment.

While the arrangement is a mere footnote in the history of Western classical music, it constitutes the very foundation of jazz. From 1920s recordings of New Orleans jazz to today's improvisatory explorations in free jazz, arrangements have been springboards to experimentation and interplay between the recognizable and the novel. Many of the amendments to America's copyright regime in the twentieth century were devised as responses to jazz covers of "standards," well-known tunes drawn from factory-like songwriting environments such as Vaudeville, Tin Pan Alley, or Broadway. Because a derivative work cannot be copyrighted without the original holder's permission, arrangements and solos in new versions of standard songs rarely earn royalties for performers and arrangers unless these parties are somehow able to negotiate an adaptation copyright with the original publishers.[21] As a result, the wealth in the jazz industry has traditionally been consolidated among the copyright holders of standards, leaving performers few opportunities to profit from transformative appropriation.

Given these formidable financial drawbacks, many arrangers have turned to the public domain for sources of free musical building blocks. Classical music, attractive to arrangers because the copyrights for most pieces have already expired, has also appealed to American listeners because of its association with elitist values such as wealth, intelligence, refined taste, religiosity, and Western European heritage.[22] Early easy-listening musicians seized upon the radio as a means of rendering arranged concert repertoire accessible to the masses. André Kostelanetz, one of the premiere "light" music arrangers of the 1930s and 1940s, performed and broadcast simplified versions of famous classical works such as Debussy's "The Girl with the Flaxen Hair." He explained his efforts as attempts to share with all classes the cultural capital that previously had been reserved for the educated and privileged. Radio made mass dissemination feasible, but not without some alterations; Kostelanetz pared down large orchestral movements to pieces lasting four or five minutes and transcribed ensemble works for solo instruments. Classical music has continued to appear in later popular music from the 1950s to the present, from arrangements of opera arias to hip-hop samplings of Beethoven's "Für Elise." Detractors regarded "pop classics" as cheap imitations that rob great works of their nobility and transcendence. Theodor Adorno, one of the most aggressive critics of mass culture in the 1930s and 1940s, complained that pop classics disregarded the integrity of great works in order to make them catchy:

> [The pop classic] blatantly snatches the reified bits and pieces out of their context and sets them up as a pot pourri. It destroys the multi-level unity of the whole work and brings forward only isolated popular passages. The minuet from Mozart's E-Flat Major Symphony, played without the other movements, loses its symphonic cohesion and is turned by the performance into an artisan-type genre piece that has more to do with the "Stephanie Gavotte" [an anodyne American pop hit from 1880s by Alphons Czibulka] than with the sort of classicism it is supposed to advertise.[23]

But what does it mean to popularize the classical? It depends on the relevance of the old work within the new work. Familiar melodies like "O sole mio" (a traditional Neapolitan song) or Bach's Minuet in G Major are themselves pleasant enough, but perhaps a bit daunting to some American listeners who may have had little exposure to European languages or to formal musical study. But the lyrics of

Elvis Presley's "It's Now or Never" (1960), set to the melody of "O sole mio," bridge that chasm by providing a familiar narrative of love and longing. The Toys' "A Lover's Concerto" (1966) changes Bach's triple-meter piano exercise into a swinging duple-meter radio tune.

Conversely, certain classical musicians have released tribute arrangements of popular works. Early-music specialist Joshua Rifkin recorded the *Baroque Beatles Book* in 1965, an album in which melodies from "I Want to Hold Your Hand," "Help!" and the like were submitted to Bach-esque contrapuntal and fugal arrangements. *Baroque Beatles* was released just as the Fab Four were charming critics and musicologists, the gatekeepers of high art music.[24] The recording legitimated the Beatles over their pop-band peers who were cast as anti-intellectual. Rifkin's album also bestowed a compliment of sorts by establishing the Beatles' songs as worthy of classical reinterpretation. Similar highbrow renditions of popular music have been undertaken with the works of more recent artists such as Radiohead (*Enigmatic: The String Quartet Tribute to Radiohead* and *Strung Out on OK Computer: The String Quartet Tribute to Radiohead*) and even Metallica (*Apocalyptica Plays Metallica By Four Cellos*).

Pop-to-classical and classical-to-pop arrangements broadcast inherent sociopolitical messages. They espouse egalitarianism by claiming that what's good for the few can be good for the many. By the same token, the musical structure of these arrangements privileges one musical aspect, almost always the melody, as the *lingua franca* to which audiences will respond. In both types of adaptation, aspects such as harmony, orchestration, rhythm, and tempo are usually altered; lyrics are often left out altogether. By doing this, the arranger identifies the melody as "timeless," relegating virtually every other musical element to the realm of the transient, ephemeral, or fashionable. Imagine alternative scenarios: a verbatim transcription of a Beethoven string quartet for electric guitar quartet, or a commercial jingle using the harmony (but not the melody) of a Bach chorale. In the former, the rigor of Beethoven would seem mismatched with the instrumentation. Without a concession to the styles and sounds of the electric guitar, such an arrangement would sound anachronistic. As to the latter example, most listeners simply would not recognize the Bach reference because we are not used to listening harmonically without the guide of a familiar melody.

Classical-to-pop arrangements first found a niche in the new market of "background" music that emerged in the 1920s, thanks to companies like Muzak. The philosophy driving Muzak was to provide exactly the right amount of familiar material, such that the attentive listener might recognize an arrangement while the distracted or occupied bystander would hardly notice the song at all. Muzak began as a wire service for which subscribers paid to have prerecorded songs piped in as background music. The product was pitched to restaurants and bars, where it could substitute for costly live entertainment. It was also available for residential use as an alternative to wireless radio. The founders of the Muzak Corporation preached the merits of background music as a workplace stimulant, an unobtrusive musical salve that would stimulate (but not distract) workers, ultimately increasing productivity.[25] Muzak's technology derived from George Owen Squier's 1910 invention of a mechanism enabling the piggybacking of multiple lines of communication over one telephone wire. This tool had obvious military applications, but Squier foresaw peacetime usage as a means of pacifying crowds. The Muzak Corporation did not invent light music, which by the 1920s had already become the largest seller in the American music market. But Muzak aimed specifically at being a purveyor of light music, providing multiple "networks" specially selected to fit certain moods and venues, from the home to the department store. In

1934 Muzak released its first self-produced recording, a medley of three tunes performed by Sam Lanin and his orchestra. For the next decade, Muzak featured classical, semi-classical, pop vocal, Polynesian, and Gypsy tunes performed by easy-listening stars. Muzak was appealing because its subscription fees already included licensing, so restaurateurs didn't have to pay a musicians' union or publishing representative such as ASCAP. And when Warner Brothers bought Muzak, it united the company with Associated Music Publishers (then the only competitor to ASCAP), granting Muzak the rights to yet other classical and semi-classical compositions.

Mood-enhancing music like Muzak and other easy-listening styles were early-twentieth-century forms of utilitarian music whose purpose was to alter human behavior. But unlike Kostelanetz arrangements, Muzak presented an enigma: music that was enjoyable but meant to be ignored. Restaurant owners who signed up for the Muzak subscription service wanted pleasant sounds that would subconsciously coax customers to stay, eat, and order drinks. Yet this experience was not the same as attending a live concert or cabaret, or even listening attentively to the radio. Muzak offered a populist's paradise in which the elitism of classical music was removed but its positive associations remained.

Just as Muzak did for previous generations, Walter Murphy's "A Fifth of Beethoven" provided a modernized, streamlined version of a well-known classic, the first movement of Beethoven's Fifth Symphony. "A Fifth" appeared on the soundtrack to the 1977 film *Saturday Night Fever*. And like Muzak, "A Fifth" also functions as a musical distraction by reusing only the most superficial feature of Beethoven's symphony, the distinctive " 'V' for Victory" theme.[26] The track begins with the dramatic string theme of the original, G–E♭–F–D–D'–C. For the first few seconds one might imagine the piece to be just another recording of the famous orchestral work, but then a drum set enters with a four-on-the-floor disco rhythm, and the music is violently dragged into the twentieth century as Beethoven's sonata allegro movement is forced into a banal verse-chorus form. The strings complement this groove by expanding their Beethovenian unison to octave voicings like those in a Thom Bell arrangement.[27] The strings are backed up with bass and rhythm guitar, horns, flutes, oboes, timpani, and even a vibraslap.[28] During the first "verse," the strings duplicate the melody of the original by restating the opening theme in several ascending sequences, each building upon the tension of the last. In Beethoven's original, these escalations act as transitional material leading to the second theme group in E♭ major. But in Murphy's "Fifth," this tension doesn't result in a harmonic migration but instead returns to the opening theme in C minor, which by now resembles the chorus of a repet-itive pop song. In the second verse, a solo organ vamps for four bars on a takeoff of the blues scale. The strings then reenter with disco-inflected flourishes: strident, modal, in parallel octaves. Then, a bridge section begins, increasing tension with transitional material in the horns that results in a satisfactory dominant-to-tonic cadence. This is the "recapitulation," so to speak. The closing bars provide a mini-coda in the form of a Neapolitan augmented sixth chord held by a fermata, then one final iteration of the theme.

More than a few listeners find "A Fifth of Beethoven" to be dis-tasteful; one critic calls it a "trivial piece of pop ephemera that may have set new standards for ephemeral triviality."[29] The track seems to desecrate its source material, foisting clichés of disco music onto a warhorse of concert music repertoire. But bad taste is perhaps pre-cisely the impression that Walter Murphy was aiming to create. The song seems ironically conscious of the solemnity of its namesake, Beethoven's Fifth Symphony, one of the most famous and recog-nizable European concert works of all time and an iconic piece that in today's popular culture symbolizes intelligence and passion.[30] "A Fifth of Beethoven" recasts Beethoven's original rhythms into what were in the late 1970s trendy disco beats. Having no veneration for its source material, "A Fifth" suffers from derision even while Walter Carlos's *Switched-On Bach* has been lauded as what Bach might have intended had he lived in the twentieth century. Released in 1968, *Switched-On Bach* is an anthology of various Bach Preludes, Fugues, and Brandenburg Concerto movements for Moog synthesizer. Walter Carlos (a transsexual who in 1979 became Wendy Carlos) received considerable critical praise for the album, even from such respected acoustic performers as Glenn Gould.[31] So, how is Murphy's Beethoven arrangement different from Carlos's Bach recordings?

Carlos's arrangement is a *transcription*; he neither added nor subtracted any notes from the original pieces, but rather performed them on a new instrument. His proponents felt that he treated Bach's work with due reverence and, on that basis alone, were willing to pardon his using new technologies that adherents to authenticity would not normally tolerate. Carlos fans were quick to point out that instrumentation during Bach's era was fluid, and that several pieces known today as being written for one instrument may have been intended for others originally. Some of Carlos's transcriptions offer something else new: tempos that are impossible for any human keyboard player to execute. To many this seems a trivial modification, whereas Murphy's "A Fifth of Beethoven" commits the unpardonable sin of changing Beethoven's *content*. But content is inseparable from the entire sound of the piece and is not limited to pitches and rhythms. "A Fifth of Beethoven" may seem flippant, but only because it changes the emotional impact of Beethoven's Fifth Symphony from tortured and dramatic to flippant. Bach's instrumental music may not have been *about* anything, but it was intended for human performance, whereas Carlos's superhuman *Switched-*

On Bach arguably departs as much from Bach as Murphy did from Beethoven.

The true difference between Murphy and Carlos concerns the intentions of the arranger. Murphy was essentially telling a musical joke, jumping on the bandwagon of fashionable disco records performed by celebrities (such as *The Ethel Merman Disco Album* or Frank Sinatra's disco version of "Night and Day") or based on commercially successful music (such as the disco medley of the *Star Wars* soundtrack). Carlos, by contrast, was the first musician to produce an electronic version of a canonical classical composition. Plus, he premiered *Switched-On Bach* to academics at a meeting of the Audio Engineering Society of New York, so his motives seemed nobler because the work was framed as academic research rather than a commercial enterprise.

COVER SONGS

Like the Murphy and Carlos examples, recorded cover songs of the blues, R&B, and rock have been the center of debates concerning musical taste and ethics. Rock-'n'-roll-era covers often engaged in the process known as "crossing over," wherein a song initially produced by members of one particular race or ethnicity becomes popular with members of another race or ethnicity. Crossover covers were popular throughout the 1950s and existed in various permutations (for example, a "white" song crossing over to the "black" market, a samba crossing over into standard white pop charts). Rock 'n' roll covers ignited moral outrage because of the financial success so many white performers achieved through the replay of songs originally written or performed by black musicians. Pat Boone's stiff send-up of Little Richard's "Tutti Frutti" and Elvis Presley's sanitized version of Big Mama Thornton's signature song "Hound

Dog" have led critics to complain that white singers replaced the spontaneity of black performances with a commercial, saccharine style. White covers may have yielded plentiful royalties for copyright holders, but their original performers seldom profited. In addition, black songwriters were sometimes forced to share writing credits with white artists in order to have their songs performed, and were frequently paid below the mechanical statutory rate for recordings of their works.[32]

Surprisingly, black musicians enjoyed some benefits from the crossover phenomenon. The practice opened up black R&B to much larger audiences, and as a result many black musicians began to garner previously unheard-of recognition and financial gain. Black R&B musicians were just as likely to cover white songs in the crossover-rich atmosphere of the mid-1950s (for example, the Orioles' hit "Crying in the Chapel" was actually a cover of a country ballad by the white singer Darrell Glenn); this improved the situation of black songwriters as BMI and independent publishing companies aggressively pursued royalties for the artists they represented.[33]

The rock 'n' roll cover debate focuses primarily on ethics rather than the law. In most instances, white artists who covered black songs adhered to copyright law by reporting authorship and paying royalties to the publisher. Baraka and Maultsby still dub the phenomenon white "raping" of black culture, even though it was often performance style (something that used to receive scant protection in the United States) rather than compositions that were appropriated. Yet responsibility for the whitewashing of black musical culture lies not only on entertainers like Elvis (who assiduously credited black musicians as his inspiration), but also with radio disk jockeys who stopped playing the first version of a song once a famous artist covered it. Most listeners did not have encyclopedic tastes in the 1950s and did not usually track the black originators of their favorite tunes, so once a white cover appeared, the black original usually disappeared from playlists and record shops. Black performers, meanwhile, were locked into exploitive contracts that limited their ability to profit from their own performances, so even those whose work had suddenly become popular were not assured royalties.

The critics of crossover covers are in many ways as deaf to musical detail as the framers of copyright law because they focus on only the most salient aspects of a composition. It's easy to track the additions and omissions of lyrics from one version to the next, but changes in tempo, instrumentation, and vocal timbre are harder to read critically. Take Elvis Presley's 1956 cover of "Lawdy Miss Clawdy," written and originally performed in 1952 by Lloyd Price. The lyrics of the cover are virtually the same as the original, so we have only the arrangements themselves to compare. Presley's cover is upbeat and peppy with his signature "nanny goat" vibrato. Price's version is slower and statelier, seemingly more resigned to its painful subject, an unfaithful girlfriend. Where Price uses a baritone sax for a solo, the Elvis version substitutes Scotty Moore's guitar solo. The differences between original and cover are analogous for another track on the same Presley album, "Shake, Rattle, and Roll," written by Charles E. Calhoun and originally recorded by Joe Turner in 1954. Elvis discards one salacious line in Turner's version mentioning a see-through dress, but otherwise he keeps the lyrics intact. Turner's version is slower than Elvis's, and like Price, Turner uses a baritone sax, which in the Elvis version is replaced with not one, but two guitar solos.

The music critic Nelson George writes that Elvis was "just a package, a performer with limited musical ambition and no real dedication to the black style that made him seem so dangerous."[34] George is right insofar that Presley borrows relatively little in terms of vocal style and instrumental arrangement from Price and Turner. His appropriations are much more straightforward, taking from the materials already protected by copyright: lyrics and melody. So unless a cover artist can be criticized for *not* imitating a respected artist's rendition, we have to reevaluate Elvis's supposed transgressions. Although many listeners prefer the original versions to Presley's, it is more difficult to claim that these were immoral or unethical covers, especially since Presley genuinely (and publicly) admired black music. If Elvis was just a poor imitator of black R&B singers, then we are really condemning him not for what he stole from black music, but for what he didn't steal, or in other words, the degree to which he "whitened up" what was originally black style. As Richard Middleton observes, Elvis's vocal performance style is a blending of blues and R&B with the mannerisms of white crooners.[35] Though Presley's early Sun and RCA recordings are admittedly indebted to black music, they also borrow from white country and gospel idioms. Yet because of the exploitation that many black performers suffered at the hands of their own agents, labels, and publishers, Presley's selective appropriations of black musical style have been interpreted by many as opportunistic and racist.

PARODY AND SATIRE

Those unsympathetic to Walter Murphy or Elvis Presley might claim that their covers lack proper respect for their source materials. When this lack of respect is communicated through instrumental, nonverbal means, the result still qualifies legally as a cover regardless of its aesthetic merits. When flippancy is conveyed through words, however, the arrangement is no longer simply a cover; its transformative nature makes it parody or satire. The *Oxford English Dictionary* describes *parody* as a composition "in which the characteristic turns of thought and phrase in an author or class of authors are imitated in such a way as to make them appear ridiculous, especially by applying them to ludicrously inappropriate subjects." A *satire* is defined as a work in which "prevailing vices or follies are held up to ridicule."[36] The difference resides in the object of ridicule: parody mocks a specific type of work or author, while satire attacks general societal ills. This distinction is not of merely academic importance but has concrete legal consequences as well. Parody has traditionally been counted as a form of criticism potentially allowed under the fair use provision of copyright law, so borrowing materials for use in a parody can potentially exempt the appropriator from licensing.[37] Satires based on copyrighted works receive no exemption and must be licensed by the original copyright holder.

The Copyright Act of 1976 lists four factors to be considered in determining whether a use of copyrighted work can be considered "fair." One factor is "the purpose and character of the use, including whether such use is of a commercial nature or is for nonprofit educational purposes."[38] Standard nonprofit activities include criticism, commentary, and reporting. The question of whether a *commercial* parody can count as fair use was answered in the Supreme Court decision on *Campbell v. Acuff-Rose Music* (1994).[39] This case concerned "Pretty Woman," a track released in 1989 by the Miami-based rap group 2 Live Crew. Luther Campbell based the song on lyrics and melodic material from the 1964 hit song "Oh, Pretty Woman," performed by Roy Orbison and cowritten by Orbison and William Dees. This lawsuit began in 1991 when Acuff-Rose Music, publishers of Orbison's "Oh, Pretty Woman," sued 2 Live Crew and its record company, Luke Skyywalker Records, for copyright infringement. The 2 Live Crew version is a low-tech cover of the Orbison original and borrows its opening guitar motive, an ascending dominant-seventh arpeggio. 2 Live Crew uses a drum machine to imitate the distinctive marchlike snare drum attacks, as well as artificial record-scratching sounds. The lyrics of 2 Live Crew's "Pretty Woman" are radically altered from Orbison's original, which praises and ultimately wins the affections of an alluring female. In 2 Live Crew's song, the subject of the lyrics is in fact not attractive, but described as hairy, bald, and unfaithful.

Soon after writing "Pretty Woman," Luther Campbell had 2 Live Crew's manager approach Acuff-Rose to announce that the group was about to release a comic rendition of the Orbison song. The group promised to credit ownership of the song to Acuff-Rose, Orbison, and Dees, and offered to pay the statutory fee for mechanical reproduction for the right to use the song. Acuff-Rose responded with a refusal to grant permission, but two days before receiving this negative reply, 2 Live Crew had already released the song on their album, As Clean As They Wanna Be. [40] Acuff-Rose then sued 2 Live Crew for copyright infringement. The District Court of Tennessee granted summary judgment to the defendants because it found that commercial parody did not preempt a fair use, that "Pretty Woman" was indeed a parody, that the borrowing from "Oh, Pretty Woman" was not excessive, and that the market for the original song would not likely be harmed by such a parody. [41]

Acuff-Rose appealed to the Sixth Circuit Court, which in 1992 reversed the decision and remanded to trial court on the basis that a commercial work cannot count as a fair use even if it is parodic. [42] Campbell then appealed to the Supreme Court, which unanimously reversed the Sixth Court's decision. The Supreme Court's findings indicate only that "commercial parody could be a fair use." [43] The court had little to say on the quality of 2 Live Crew's parody beyond affirming that the borrowing was not excessive. The Campbell decision broke new ground, affirming that a borrowing within a commercial work can still qualify as a fair use if other factors do not indicate excessive or damaging dependence on the original source. However, this ruling also remanded to trial court, meaning that it ordered the District Court to implement the Supreme Court's theoretical findings in order to decide whether 2 Live Crew's song specifically counted as a fair use. Perhaps because lawyers' fees had exhausted their bank accounts, the litigants settled out of court before the next trial phase could commence.

Curiously, 2 Live Crew initially identified its "Pretty Woman" not as a parody at all, but rather a cover that satirized the original.[44] Only after the lawsuit was filed did the group claim its song as a fair use not requiring licensing at all. But if "Pretty Woman" really were only a cover, 2 Live Crew could simply have paid the statutory mechanical reproduction license and reported the use. That the group asked permission from Acuff-Rose indicates that 2 Live Crew doubted the legality of its "cover." If "Pretty Woman" had returned to trial court, it might well have been interpreted as parody. The song's legal status on this basis alone was quite different from works by a musical satirist like Weird Al Yankovic, who has made a career out of lampooning popular songs. Yankovic's imitations like "Eat It" (based on Michael Jackson's "Beat It") or "King of Suede" (based on the Police's "King of Pain") list both Yankovic and the original songwriters, Michael Jackson and Sting respectively. But because the lyrics of Yankovic's imitations depart significantly from the originals, he cannot qualify for a compulsory mechanical reproduction license since his works are not strictly "covers." Yet they are not parodies either. A song like "Eat It" uses the Jackson original simply as a point of departure, but it does not make fun of the themes or values expressed in the original. These songs count as satire rather than parody, and Yankovic accordingly has no choice but to solicit authorization for his appropriations. He has often convinced publishers and artists that his songs pose no threat to the originals, and because of this (and the fact that his recordings tend to sell well) he has generally succeeded at acquiring licenses.

Parody and satire are audibly different in instances of music that has lyrics. But significant alterations to song lyrics prevent an appropriator from relying on compulsory licensing. The appropriator must seek permission directly from the publisher in order to use the work. There is always the chance that licensing could be denied, as it was in Acuff-Rose's rejection of 2 Live Crew's request. Still other forms of musical parody can never qualify for the parody fair-use exemption because they rely on nonverbal means to convey humor or mockery. One such example is a Mike Flowers cover of "Wonderwall," a 1995 tune originally written and performed by the British rock band Oasis. This song is technically a cover because it retains the original's lyrics and melody, so Mike Flowers could freely record his own arrangement by simply crediting Oasis's songwriter Noel Gallagher and listing Sony Music as the original publisher. But the affective distance between the original and cover is so great that we cannot hear the cover as a mere arrangement or tribute. Flowers's purely musical transformations communicate mockery in the same way that 2 Live Crew's lyrics for "Pretty Woman" mocked Orbison's "Oh, Pretty Woman."

Oasis enjoyed success during the mid-1990s as a British rock band frequently likened to the Rolling Stones and the Beatles. Noel Gallagher explained his goals with Oasis as follows: "With every song that I write, I compare it to the Beatles. I've got semi-close once or twice [. . .] if I'd been born at the same time as John Lennon, I'd have been up there."[45] The track "Wonderwall" appears on the album *(What's The Story) Morning Glory*, whose photos are visual quotations of Beatles publicity materials. The front cover of *Morning Glory* features two band members walking across a street in a manner reminiscent of the famous *Abbey Road* cover. An inside close-up shows Gallagher with a mop-top haircut and turtleneck sweater, similar to photos of John Lennon during the *Help!* era, around 1967. Even the song title "Wonderwall" comes from the eponymous 1968 film with a soundtrack by George Harrison. Oasis's devotion to the Beatles seems to have made the band a perfect target for the lounge parody of Mike Flowers, who was also fairly popular in the United Kingdom during the mid-1990s. Mike Flowers is best known for "Call Me," his contribution to the soundtrack for the movie *Austin Powers: International Man of Mystery* (1997). He took part in a lounge revival movement that celebrated easy-listening and hi-fi music from the early 1960s, and his music (both covers and original compositions) features smooth singing with cha-cha rhythms and space-age bachelor pad orchestration.[46] Lounge revival songs are anything but earnest. They celebrate swinging lifestyles and hedonism, but shy away from sentimentality and confessional self-discovery.

Flowers's cover of "Wonderwall" begins with the pops and scratches of a vinyl disc (like those on 2 Live Crew's "Pretty Woman"), as if the song is being played from an old record. The instrumental music begins with a guitar riff composed of the same pitches (B–D–F♯–E) used in the ending piano motive of the Oasis original. This is a musical wink; Mike Flowers is *literally* beginning where Oasis left off. Next, synthesized flutes, horns, bass, and a Latin rhythm section join the guitar, but these materials are pure lounge, bearing no resemblance to Oasis's music. The funniest moment occurs when Mike Flowers begins singing. His words are the same as Gallagher's, but Flowers has a velvety baritone modeled on Dean Martin and Sammy Davis Jr., whereas Gallagher sings in the pinched, raw style of a rock singer who is trying to convince the audience of his sincerity. Flowers's "Wonderwall" reached number two on the United Kingdom pop charts in December 1995, actually surpassing Oasis's version. This is by no account the first time that a cover has exceeded the success of an original song, but unlike many R&B

groups whose songs were covered by whites during the rock 'n' roll era, Oasis did not suffer from obscurity. Next to the perky urbanity of the Flowers cover, the Oasis original seems to take itself much too seriously. Flowers probably would have encountered legal and financial challenges had he chosen to satirize or parody Oasis through lyrics, but instead he maintained leeway for himself by confining his critique to nonverbal musical elements.[47]

COMMODIFYING PERFORMANCE STYLE AND VOICE

The examples listed above involve works that borrow from lyrics or melodies. In principle, these facets of musical expression are protected under the U.S. copyright regime, but as we saw above, questions of ownership are moot if the original work is in the public domain. With the Elvis Presley and Mike Flowers covers, the aspects that made these works most remarkable were not their lyrical and melodic appropriations, but rather what they borrowed in terms of musical *style*. Elvis has been criticized for borrowing the surface characteristics of black R&B without conveying the substance of the originals. Mike Flowers mocked Oasis by retaining melody and lyrics while substituting an easy-listening lounge style in place of the original version's rock idiom. These cases point to the fact that much of the affective impact of a piece of music resides in performance style, something that receives no protection under federal law. Anyone who has heard the difference between Little Richard's and Pat Boone's versions of "Tutti Frutti" can attest to the fact that performance style makes all the difference between a compelling interpretation and a rendition that falls flat.

Famous entertainers and celebrities have succeeded in the past few decades in increasing protection for aspects of their personas that still lack coverage under statutory copyright law, such as vocal characteristics and performance style. Three pivotal cases involve well-known musicians: Nancy Sinatra, Bette Midler, and Tom Waits. All three sued companies for hiring singers to imitate their distinctive vocal styles in television or radio commercials. Yet these cases were prosecuted using different strategies and encountered varying degrees of success, largely because the law's treatment of performers' rights has evolved considerably in the past thirty years. Nancy Sinatra litigated in 1970, when performers' rights were virtually nonexistent; Bette Midler in 1988, when the right of publicity was gaining strength in California law; and Tom Waits in 1991, when his counsel could refer to laws and to precedent-setting trial outcomes that defended performers' rights separately from those of authors or composers. With three different ways of arguing the same essential complaint, we see that in the courtroom, as in the recording studio, style and timing are everything.

In 1970 Nancy Sinatra sued Goodyear Tire and Rubber Company for producing a series of radio and television commercials that featured four Sinatra look-alikes, complete with her "mod"-fashion mini-skirts and go-go boots.[48] The commercials featured an off-screen voice singing the words "These boots." The defendants admitted that this invisible singer was hired to imitate Sinatra's performance of her 1965 signature song, "These Boots Are Made for Walkin'." Sinatra's counsel accused Goodyear of three misdeeds: stealing a "performance style," infringing on a "secondary meaning" of Sinatra's voice, and passing off Sinatra's celebrity identity in order to sell a product. Sinatra lost at both the District Court and Court of Appeals levels, but the questions posed by her counsel were to reappear in subsequent lawsuits involving musical impersonations. Regarding the first issue, Sinatra argued that her arrangement and performance of the song belonged to her and that only she had the right to decide whether to sell them. But the defense noted that the

Copyright Act makes no mention of performers' rights, only those of composers, arrangers, and publishers. Prior to the appearance of the advertisement, however, Young and Rubicam, the advertising agency hired to produce the commercials, had entered into a licensing agreement with the publisher of "These Boots Are Made for Walkin'," who granted rights to arrange the song for commercial publicity over television and radio. Because Sinatra herself did not own the copyright to the song in question, she could not prevent others from referring to its lyrics or copying her performance style, so long as they did not actually reuse her recording.

"Secondary meaning" is a term that originated within the context of American trademark law but began to appear in mid-twentieth-century discourse involving celebrity rights to privacy and control over their images. The primary meaning of the word "apple" refers to the fruit, but when used within the context of digital technology, the word's secondary meaning pertains to a specific brand of computer. Usually secondary meaning is attributed to things that are clearly discernable, definable, or tangible (e.g., the image of a famous actor, the stand-up routine of a comedian, or the signature of a politician). In the second prong to her complaint, Sinatra tried to claim that her voice, particularly when singing "These Boots," had acquired an iconic status such that the sound of the song immediately connoted the *presence* of Nancy Sinatra. By hiring a singer to perform Sinatra's signature song while impersonating her voice, Goodyear was abusing the secondary meaning that Sinatra had constructed. Until quite recently, courts have been leery of including musical sounds in this grouping. As Jane Gaines writes in her assessment of *Sinatra v. Goodyear*:

> The court's reluctance to protect the performer's voice has to do less with legal magnanimity than with a cultural perception of sound as

unprotectable because of its essential "propertyless" condition. For in
order to establish secondary meaning in one sound, a proprietor must
establish its distinctiveness from other sounds. Or, to go the other route
and attempt to establish a copyright claim, a proprietor must distinguish the performer's contribution from those of composers, lyricists,
instrumentalists, arrangers, and authors.[49]

This statement should be qualified slightly: even by 1970, laws in the
United States *had* deemed that under certain circumstances sounds
could possess secondary meaning and thus could be considered as
property. Such cases involved not original compositions, but rather
aural trademarks like MGM's lion's roar or the NBC chime. In these
instances, a brief unmistakable sound had been used in tandem with
a corporate logo or title so that the sound became synonymous with
a certain company's name. Nancy Sinatra, on the other hand, was
hardly a corporation, but simply a popular singer whose style was,
though unique, not entirely distinguishable from other musicians.
For the Ninth Circuit Court in 1970, Sinatra's sound, while recognizable, did not possess the instant "brand name recognition" that
NBC did. Hypothetically, CBS would be violating NBC's trademark
if it played the same chime during one of its own broadcasts. As long
as the pitches were identical, a viewer would automatically think of
NBC and might attribute the CBS program to the other network.
Yet in Sinatra's case, a licensed reperformance of "These Boots" was
allowed to approximate the original record as closely as possible,
because Sinatra's style lacked protectable legal status.

In the third part of her complaint, Sinatra alleged that Goodyear
engaged in the passing off of another singer's style as her own in order
to increase sales of their tire product, creating "unfair competition."
Laws against unfair competition do not exist at the federal level,
but some such provisions are included in the legal codes of several

states. The Ninth Circuit Court relied on California's unfair competition laws since both the plaintiff and the defendant engaged in significant professional activities in that state. The Court found for the defendant on this issue as well because Sinatra did not compete in the same industry as Goodyear, so she could not prove that she had lost listeners as a result of any confusion the commercials posed.

While Sinatra was unsuccessful in engaging federal law in favor of her suit, Bette Midler and Tom Waits successfully proved violations of state and federal laws protecting their voices. In 1988 Bette Midler filed suit against Ford Motor Company for imitating her voice in a television commercial; Midler lost at the district court level but won at the Ninth Circuit Court of Appeals.[50] The advertising firm Young and Rubicam was again responsible for the commercial, and just as they had done with their Goodyear publicities, they had already secured licensing from the publishers of "Do You Want to Dance," the song that was arranged for the Ford ad. Midler's counsel was well aware of the daunting precedent set by *Sinatra v. Goodyear* and, with that in mind, honed in on only one of the three elements that played into the Goodyear ruling. Midler's lawyers acknowledged that her voice did not possess secondary meaning, and they did not try to claim that the Ford commercial was passing off another singer as Midler. Instead, they successfully proved that Midler's voice (rather than her performance style in any *particular* song) was her property, even if the song Ford used did not belong to her. Again, state law was invoked in the absence of any federal law. Section 990(b), a 1985 amendment to the California Civil Code, "offers statutory protection to the voice, signature, photograph, or likeness of a deceased celebrity."[51] The Ninth Circuit Court acknowledged that while this law technically pertained to dead entertainers, its very existence proved that celebrity likenesses were protectable, and could therefore be protectable for living entertainers as well.

In 1991 Tom Waits successfully sued Frito-Lay for imitating his voice in television commercials advertising "Salsa Rio"–flavored Doritos snack chips.[52] Waits echoed Midler's accusation of voice misappropriation under Section 990(b) of California Code, but he also alleged that Frito-Lay was guilty of false endorsement as defined in the Lanham Act, a federal law controlling the registration and maintenance of trademarks. Waits's counsel argued that the Doritos imitation suggested to listeners that he himself had sung for the commercial. Prior to this, Waits had publicly stated that artists lost their integrity when they participated in commercials. So where Sinatra was bogged down by having to prove that Goodyear threatened her own market, the Lanham Act allowed Waits to bypass market concerns altogether, confining the issue to his reputation and the harm done to it by the Doritos ad. Waits won at both the District Court and Ninth Circuit Court of Appeals.

Midler and Waits both relied on a statute that was initially available only to the estates of deceased entertainers, the right of publicity. This idea developed in the twentieth century to protect celebrities whose images and performance styles were posthumously appropriated for marketing purposes. The right of publicity pertains to intangibles that federal copyright normally overlooks, such as a likeness, a voice, or even a "shtick" like the famous "Heeeeeeeere's Johnny" exclamation that began every episode of *The Tonight Show Starring Johnny Carson*.[53] Each state decides individually whether to adopt the right of publicity into its civil code. Not surprisingly, California civil code recognizes rights of publicity because so many entertainers and musicians reside there; Tennessee has also adopted a right of publicity after lobbying efforts on the part of Elvis Presley Enterprises.[54] The right of publicity speaks to a need among celebrities to control the dissemination of their images. If this were just about money, then Waits, Midler, and Sinatra may have accepted the offers made by these companies to participate in commercials. But during the 1970s and 1980s, celebrity endorsement was not as common as it is today. Entertainers appeared in commercials when they could no longer perform in more lucrative gigs like music recordings or films. Midler's lawsuit attempted to counteract the perception that she was past her prime. Waits was afraid that his audiences would think he had "sold out" to corporate interests after insisting on his artistic autonomy.

Moral rights have begun to inform both copyright law and other forms of intellectual property law, like the right of publicity, allowing authors control over not only the economic life of their creative output, but also the circumstances under which their work is viewed, used, and appropriated. The right of publicity endows proprietary status over elements that used to be free, so it's not surprising that many American entertainers enthusiastically endorse it. But the drawback to the right of publicity is that it bestows property status to things that might best be considered outside the realm of ownership. If James Brown tried to claim ownership of every shriek or shout not merely sampled but *inspired* by his funk albums, many musicians would find themselves at the business end of a lawsuit.

When the Fat Boys sued Joe Piscopo and Miller Brewing Company in a similar instance of celebrity imitation, their case involved trademark law, rights of publicity, and copyright. The Fat Boys embraced an explicitly anti-drug and anti-alcohol stance, and refused when Miller approached them in 1987 to participate in a new television commercial. Miller eventually secured comedian Joe Piscopo to imitate the Fat Boys, resulting in an ad showing garishly dressed hip-hop poseurs rapping syllables "brrr" and "hugga hugga" while extolling the virtues of beer. The plaintiffs argued that these syllables were significant features of a copyrighted composition that had been recorded and publicly distributed, and that the resulting association between the rappers and alcohol harmed the Fat Boys' reputation. The case idled in legal limbo from 1990 to 1994 as the defendants repeatedly challenged the legitimacy of the case, but in two separate hearings a New York District Court judge determined that there was enough of a case to go to trial.[55] After the 1994 hearing, the parties settled out of court. The plaintiffs charged Miller and Piscopo with copyright infringement of a composition and sound recording, Lanham Act violations of misleading the public with a false endorsement, unfair competition, and violations to rights of privacy and publicity. Had this case involved issues pertaining exclusively to performance style and celebrity identity, Miller probably would have gone to court. But the Fat Boys had affidavits from musicologists stating that Miller had clearly sampled, not imitated, the rap duo. Ethically, the Miller commercial was not fundamentally different from the Goodyear, Ford, or Frito-Lay appropriations, yet Miller's position was much weaker because it had infringed not only on performance style but on a composition as well.

Eminem's 2004 lawsuit over a television advertisement further demonstrates the clout of celebrity identity in the courtroom. Eminem sued Apple Computer and MTV for $10 million in damages for using his song "Lose Yourself" in an ad for iTunes without permission. This lawsuit alleges straightforward copyright infringement, yet Eminem's counsel describes "Lose Yourself" as possessing "iconic stature" and points to Eminem's avoidance of product endorsement as testimony to the gravity of the alleged infringement.[56] The Midler and Waits cases established these same sorts of arguments in an explicitly non-copyright context, and their success explains why these justifications are now being used to buttress what is presumably a classic example of copyright infringement through unauthorized rebroadcast.

Waits v. Frito-Lay and *Midler v. Ford* indicate that a singer who is famous enough to be recognized by his or her voice alone can protect that voice from being appropriated or mimicked without permission. Musical impersonation cases may become more common as new technologies allow for increasing degrees of fidelity in vocal imitation. Until recently, synthesizers could render musical instruments reasonably well, but the human voice, with its subtly distinctive phonemes and tonal variations, was too difficult to produce with anything beyond a robotic monotone. The Vocaloid, a new software developed by the Yamaha Corporation, has overcome this challenge.[57] The program contains thousands of individual vowels and consonants performed by a real singer. The user specifies syllables, words, pitches, and rhythms, and the software produces continuous melody indistinguishable from the singing of a human being. In late 2003 when the Vocaloid was first primed for release, the software was programmed to produce only one *style* of singing: soul. But developers were already working to make other styles such as country, metal, and classical available for purchase.

With today's level of technology, the user can produce only the performance style of the singer who actually recorded his or her own voice into the Vocaloid. But given the exponential rate of increase in software sophistication, it is only a matter of time before the Vocaloid and similar voice synthesis programs imitate voices that were not fed into it. This has obvious applications in the commercial arena, where celebrity voices could be re-created for the purpose of hawking products. This technology raises provocative legal questions. Imagine a hypothetical situation in which McDonald's uses a vocal synthesis program to create an imitation of Frank Sinatra's voice for a jingle about hamburgers. If the Frank Sinatra Estate were to object to the imitation, would it have a viable complaint in the courts? And who would be the target of a lawsuit: McDonald's, the manufacturers of the software, or both? Many synthesizers currently available contain precleared samples, meaning that the originators of the sounds have issued general licenses allowing for any usage. But with the next stage of acoustics technology, sampling may become passé as musicians begin to use reconstituted digital allusions to their favorite entertainers.

A CENTURY OF ELVIS

Elvis Presley's postmortem body and voice are animated by the tensions characterizing the musical appropriation debates of the twentieth century. For his detractors, Elvis's crime was being at the right place at the right time, a white artist who could profit from the innovations of Chuck Berry and Little Richard. Elvis is a central figure in discussions of musical allusion not only because of what he did, but also because of what he symbolizes. For some listeners, Elvis is the most successful example of "blackface," a type of nineteenth-century stage entertainment in which both white and black actors, their faces darkened with burnt coal, presented stereotypes of black life on the plantation and in the city. Blackface persisted into the twentieth century with Al Jolson's performance in *The Jazz Singer*. Traces of it can be seen in early Warner Brothers cartoons, television shows like *Amos and Andy*, blaxploitation cinema, and even the dance moves of Michael Jackson and MC Hammer. [58] Regardless of whether Elvis viewed African American culture as worthy of respect or just as raw material for his own stage persona, he engaged in blackface by presenting to white audiences titillating glimpses (and distortions) of black culture. Elvis's many covers and tributes to black music usually gloss over the less desirable sides of African American life such as poverty and racism.

Presley's treatment of black culture, in other words, is not at all unique in a tradition of repeated white appropriations of black culture. Rather, the coinciding of the rock 'n' roll movement with the civil rights movement made Presley morally suspect and redefined blackface by changing the very status of musical and cultural appropriation. As the South struggled with integration, listeners began to examine the meaning of the sights and sounds of black culture that previously went unquestioned. Presley encounters criticism today not because of what he did, but because of how our society has changed. In the nineteenth century, style and performance (and even compositions themselves) were not as anchored in notions of property and ownership as they are now. Thanks to the civil rights movement and the increasing influence of moral rights in intellectual property, we now tend to think of performance style as *belonging* to its originator.

Elvis is the quintessential figure of allusive appropriation not only for his own borrowings and thefts, but also for the myriad appropriations of Elvis that permeate modern culture. Most of these appropriations are only tangentially musical. Elvis's silhouette in the 1993 film *True Romance* offers advice to the protagonist, but his onscreen presence consists of only a few hip wiggles. Elvis's image appears on postage stamps and his imitators fill Las Vegas nightclubs and wedding chapels, all under the watchful eye of EPE. The identity of Elvis is one of the most heavily protected commodities in the world. And EPE is thriving by marketing the King's image through a variety of different media. With this in mind, we can listen better to Elvis's resurrected voice in the 2002 remix of "A Little Less Conversation" by JXL (the stage name for Dutch DJ Holkenburg). This version, which sets Elvis's original lyrics to electronica backup, scored high on the UK charts. The song is striking because of the novelty of hearing Elvis's expired voice alive again in a hip new electronica format. But what does this bit of Elvis mean in terms of intellectual property and musical appropriation?

"A Little Less Conversation" is not a conventional cover song; it's not an allusion at all, in fact, but rather a duplication of Elvis's vocals set to a new accompaniment. To release this song, JXL had to obtain licensing permission not only from the publishers (in this case, Cherry River Music and Chrysalis Songs) but also from the record label (RCA) that owned the master recordings of the song. As part of the licensing agreement, JXL yielded full publishing rights to the EPE and also agreed to be known as JXL rather than by his previous appellation, Junkie XL, which EPE felt to be in bad taste given the fact that Elvis's fatal heart failure is commonly attributed to his obesity and drug use. For all the novelty of Elvis's new techno digs, we are already used to the idea of Elvis on black velvet, Elvis imitators, and Elvis covers. So it's difficult not to simply lump the JXL remix together with the myriad examples of Elvis allusion. Discerning the difference between allusion and copying is becoming increasingly difficult. And content providers are counting on this confusion as a way of shoring up control over their property.

CHAPTER THREE

Duplication

Walter Benjamin, ruminating on the rise of mass reproduction, observes that facsimiles lack the "aura" that once characterized art: "That which withers in the age of mechanical reproduction is the aura of the work of art. [. . .] One might generalize by saying: the technique of reproduction detaches the reproduced object from the domain of tradition."[1] Benjamin defines aura as the inapproachability, uniqueness, and sense of authenticity that an old painting or recording possesses. A work possessing aura makes us shiver with the feeling that we are confronting art intimately associated with past rituals or customs. We experience the absence of aura every time we see a reproduction of a famous work like Leonardo da Vinci's *Mona Lisa*. Although the painting is well known, its reproduction on the Internet or in a book hardly induces awe. Global communication technology has enabled the dissemination of an astounding array of images, writings, and sounds. But this inundation with creative material has dulled our sensibilities to the point where we no longer feel awe when faced with a copy of a masterpiece.

Most legislators have not read Benjamin, and if they have, they were not sufficiently convinced to translate his findings into law. According to the rules of copyright, unauthorized reproductions of protected works are illegal, even if these reproductions are less-than-perfect copies. An art history professor, for instance, may not publish her own photograph of a Mark Rothko painting without licensing, even if the photo were grainy or distorted. Nobody would be fooled into believing that her photo was the real Rothko work, and yet copyright would still forbid her from reprinting the image.

Benjamin's "Work of Art" article routinely appears in discussions of digital sampling, primarily because Benjamin's observations regarding visual reproductions seem to anticipate later developments in recording technology.[2] Sounds, like paintings or photographs, can also possess aura. Listeners encounter this aura when they play dusty vinyl records and notice their pops and scratches, noises that are usually absent in digitally recorded music. Copyright law is unstinting in its insistence that reproductions, especially sound recordings, be controlled. This protectionism implies that Benjamin's findings are now outdated: reproduction does not diminish or destroy the aura, at least not in music. In the twenty-first century, we are surrounded by musical genres that involve (if not revolve around) the duplication of other recordings. Musical allusion is admittedly alive and well, but musical duplication is by far the dominant form of appropriation today. Recording equipment used to be expensive and difficult to operate without extensive training. Today, anyone willing to spend $50 on software can record and mix professional-quality tracks on a home computer. And the sound duplications created by such equipment can achieve any desired level of fidelity, from that of an amateur bootleg to a perfect sonic replica. So from today's vantage point, recordings are less like auratic objects and more like Jean Baudrillard's simulacra: infinite, perfectly identical copies with no authoritative original.[3]

Musicians encounter a relatively straightforward licensing procedure if they wish to release sound-alike versions of their favorite recordings. But the reuse of a recording, if allowed at all, can cost dearly, and those who reuse without permission risk legal penalties. Music recordings have existed since the late 1800s, but only recently has the sophistication of sound reproduction technology challenged the foundations of copyright law by enabling flawless electronic duplication. Today's laws concerning recordings are the culmination of different moments in the history of "musical collage," from *musique concrète* and the European-American post–World War II avant-garde to pop novelty collages and hip-hop sampling. Musical collage refers to any creative activity involving the duplication of preexisting recordings in part or in whole. Through its various incarnations, musical collage has enabled artists to engage diverse aesthetic and philosophical platforms. The meaning of some collage pieces is contingent upon the meanings of their constituent materials; other collage pieces allow materials to convey meanings entirely different from their original sources. Methods of treating collage materials have been intimately connected to the evolution of music as an intellectual property.

MUSIQUE CONCRÈTE AND JOHN CAGE

Musique concrète was the brainchild of Pierre Schaeffer, a Radiodiffusion France engineer whose works challenged the definition of noise.[4] Schaeffer recast prerecorded sounds by manipulating the speed and direction of turntables and magnetic tape. In 1948, the live broadcast of Schaeffer's "Concert of Noises" featured sounds of vehicles, musical instruments, and toys. He assembled his *Étude aux chemins de fer* ("Railroad Study," 1948) from various train noises, from the locomotive engine to the engineer's bell. With his sonic collages, Schaeffer was among the first to foreground the arbitrary distinctions between sound, music, and noise, a task that would preoccupy subsequent avant-garde and pop artists.

Schaeffer's turntable and tape collages consisted of disparate sounds and noises, some of which were recognizable. Yet Schaeffer urged his listeners to ignore any "residual signification" (original meanings or associations) that lingered with these sounds.[5] Integral serialist composer Pierre Boulez disparaged musique concrète because despite Schaeffer's wishes, many of its constituent materials were too closely associated with their origins. For Boulez, serious music had to be entirely abstract; materials could not possess any meanings apart from those intended by the composer. Pierre Henry, one of Schaeffer's collaborators, pursued an alternative strategy. He maintained that residual signification was not only inevitable, but of central importance in the creation of a collage. Later composers of musique concrète included Karlheinz Stockhausen, whose *Konkrete Etüde* (1952) appropriated found "sonic objects" to create nonreferential music. But by the late 1960s, Stockhausen began to assimilate Henry's aesthetics with *Telemusik* (1966) and *Hymnen* (1966–69), two works that relied on recognizable sources (non-Western music for the former, various national anthems for the latter).

Musique concrète lost momentum in the wake of Boulez's criticism precisely because its most die-hard advocates could not ignore the phenomenon of listener recognition. Schaeffer and his colleagues hoped for the audience equivalent of unbiased jurors, listeners who either were ignorant of the origins of collage materials or else were able to disregard those origins through sheer force of will. The listening experience imagined by Schaeffer was one in which all relationships and meanings existed only within the piece itself, which would ideally have no external associations. This can be a tall order, especially for Edgar Varèse's tape piece *Poème électronique* (1957–58), written after Varèse spent time with Schaeffer at the Radiodiffusion-Télévision Française studios. The *Poème* is composed primarily of sine wave distortions and industrial noises. But slightly more than halfway through, a new sound enters: a recording of a bel canto soprano, a human voice. Even more than Schaeffer's concrète pieces, the *Poème* presents if not a clear program, then at least a potential narrative premise, a contrast between the mechanical and the human. Herein lies the trouble: in searching for "meaning" behind musique concrète, how do we balance the composer's intentions with our own interpretations of the sounds we hear? Varèse's music challenges us to listen to the intrinsic qualities of both human- and mechanically produced noise; the sources of the borrowed sounds need not impinge on our understanding of the work. One wonders whether, when the *Poème* was premiered in the Philips Pavilion (designed by the postmodern architect Le Corbusier at the Brussels Exposition Universelle in 1958), listeners were tempted to interpret the *Poème* as a rumination on modernity, or even a dramatization of the potential conflict between nature and industry.

John Cage's radio pieces serve as useful points of comparison with musique concrète because they propose a radically different approach toward musical meaning. Cage's studies with Henry Cowell and Arnold Schoenberg in the 1930s cultivated his interest in non-Western music and new technologies for sound production. In 1937, Cage wrote "The Future of Music (Credo)," an essay predicting an era when technology could reproduce any sound. His pieces from this period feature wave oscillators, amplified contact mikes and variable-speed turntables. Cage's "radio compositions" encouraged performers and listeners not to exclude unplanned events as peripheral noise. In *Imaginary Landscapes No. 4* (1951), performers "play" twelve radios by tuning them to indicated frequencies at specific moments. Because radio stations are regional, *Imaginary Landscapes No. 4* almost always ensures a combination of static, half-audible, and clearly received transmissions of news, talk shows, and/or music. The work also challenges listeners by subjecting them to potential irritants such as radio static. Unlike Schaeffer, however, Cage had no expectations of how audiences would react to these sounds.

Schaeffer and Varèse were perhaps unrealistic in expecting listeners to disregard external associations. The continuing relevance of Pierre Henry's and John Cage's music among today's popular musicians is attributable to their tolerance for audience interpretation.[6] For Henry and Cage, musical collages convey multiple meanings, including those unintended by the composer. The juxtaposition of different materials in a collage can also create meanings that might not exist if each constituent work were heard separately. In the realm of sonic collage, the whole is greater than the sum of its parts. This statement may seem self-evident by twenty-first-century standards, but it is crucial to remember if we are to make the formidable aesthetic jump from musique concrète to collage in popular music. The twentieth-century experimental avant-garde was the first movement to explore the potentials of recording technology. Yet composers and musicians outside of European-American concert music have been more willing to gamble with elements that elude the composer's control: residual significance and audience interpretation. Residual significance implies (if not demands) the presence of recognizable materials, many of which are familiar because they have been released to the public as copyrighted material. This explains why avant-garde collage artists encounter no legal difficulties with their appropriations, while pop collage musicians have been plagued by IP woes from the onset.

POP COLLAGE, NOVELTIES, AND REMIXES

Dickie Goodman was the first pop artist to create a commercially successful audio collage.[7] The work was "The Flying Saucer" (1956), a knockoff of Orson Welles's "War of the Worlds" radio broadcast, during which Welles succeeded in convincing some listeners that Earth was being invaded by Martians. But Goodman's "The Flying

Saucer" is explicitly farcical, stringing together panicked reportage of the invasion with sound bites from recent rock 'n' roll recordings. For instance, a journalist tells listeners that they are about to hear the first words of a Martian. Goodman then splices in "a wop bop a loo mop a lop bam boom," the refrain from Little Richard's "Tutti Frutti." Goodman took a cue from Alan Freed, the disk jockey whose celebrity nearly matched that of the rock 'n' roll musicians featured on his radio shows. Freed was able to construct whole evenings of entertainment through assembling individual songs into cohesive shows. More importantly, Freed's commentary between songs and the very choice of songs itself propagated the myth of rock 'n' roll: that it sprung fully formed into American living rooms, that it shared nothing with previous forms of music, and that it was taking over the world. Goodman assumed Freed's position as a storyteller but used short audio clips rather than entire songs. The result was a type of musical comedy that is funny and accessible, but only to listeners already familiar with his collage source materials. "The Flying Saucer" inspired several other musical collage novelty records. This success did not endear Goodman to those in the music industry who thought he was scavenging off the labors of others. The Harry Fox Agency, which supervises mechanical licensing fees for several record companies, sued Goodman for copyright infringement. After attempts to negotiate royalties for "The Flying Saucer" failed, a New York District Court judge threw out the case, claiming that there was no evidence that "The Flying Saucer" posed any threat to the market for the original songs. Subsequent Goodman novelty releases were cleared ahead of time with publishers and record companies, who were glad to receive royalties from these lucrative records.

Dickie Goodman's novelty collages anticipate the later phenomenon of remixes, a broad term pertaining to any altered version of a song. Remixes began in reggae concerts and, later, disco clubs where a disk jockey (DJ) would use faders and echo effects to bring out specific qualities of a song. Digital samplers allowed DJs to make more sophisticated remixes, so by the 1980s it was fashionable to remix Top 40 or rock tunes into dance versions by highlighting their rhythm breaks or adding extended instrumental sections. Remixing is sometimes an adversarial enterprise in which two songs are pitted against each other in a sort of competition. Mash-ups, the latest strain of remixes, feature well-known songs that are digitally synchronized and juxtaposed so that the lyrics to one song are set to the backup instruments of another.[8] Just like Dickie Goodman's "The Flying Saucer," mash-ups began as an underground illegal phenomenon. They circulate through file transfer over the Internet and are difficult to trace. Most mash-ups feature unlikely combinations of indie pop, hip-hop, and Top 40 hits. In 2003 the most celebrated mash-ups pitted the vocals of Destiny Child's "Bootylicious" against the instruments of Nirvana's "Smells Like Teen Spirit," Céline Dion with Sigur Rós, and Herb Alpert with Public Enemy. In an attempt to recoup copyright royalty losses, some record labels have taken to selling legal versions of mash-ups for which all materials have been pre-cleared, but most aficionados scorn these as trite and commercial.

Schaeffer and Varèse conceived of a music for which collage techniques could be employed without any residual contexts bleeding into the new work. John Cage aimed at the other extreme: his collage radio broadcasts were intended to remove the composer completely from the process, leaving the listener to appreciate the sounds in and of themselves. Pierre Henry and Dickie Goodman bridged these poles by exerting a certain amount of control in assembling the pieces, yet counting on the original contexts and meanings to emerge. Working with other artists' sounds, a collage composer reveals much about his own listening process and relationships to borrowed materials. For this reason, it's helpful to think of remixes and

Henry-inspired collages as musical forms of "fan fiction," amateur creative writing and artistic productions that are loosely modeled on popular television and films.[9] Fan fiction and mash-ups are transformative appropriations in which audiences co-opt cultural icons in order to pay them homage. Implicit in both musical collage and fan fiction cultures is the concept of the "public life" of a work: once a work has been created and released to the public, it ceases to be the sole property of its creator.

COLLAGE AND HOMAGE

"Revolution 9" (1968) was the Beatles' most adventuresome collage piece and perhaps the riskiest song they ever released. Composed by John Lennon with considerable contributions from Yoko Ono, the song is a tape splicing of language instruction recordings, electroacoustic and classical music, and nonsensical babbling. By itself, "Revolution 9" would probably have gone unnoticed. But within the context of the *White Album,* the track was guaranteed at least some attention, especially in the pre-compact-disc era when one could not simply press a button to advance to the next song.

"Revolution 9" did not succeed in making contemporary art music fashionable or sexy. But the work did fuse a pop song with a musique concrète tape piece, two distinct genres with divergent aesthetic aims. "Revolution 9" reflected Lennon's growing interest (thanks to Ono) in the musical and artistic avant-garde of the middle century. The piece is conceptually indebted to Stockhausen's electroacoustic pieces because it features electronically produced sounds combined with tape collage. "Revolution 9" seemed anomalous to many Beatles fans because it clashed with Lennon's otherwise consistent output of pop songs with accessible melodies. Inspired by the series paintings of such abstract expressionists as Robert Rauschenberg and Jasper Johns, Lennon presented three musical revolutions, each one increasingly distant from the pop music status quo. The first "Revolution" was simply a great rock tune with an optimistic political message.[10] "Revolution 1" recast those lyrics in a psychedelic torpor. "Revolution 9" discarded them almost completely; the only remaining traces are intermittent fragments of Lennon singing (and eventually screaming) "alright," which occurs in the refrain of "Revolution" ("don't you know it's gonna be alright").

For anyone in tune with contemporary music trends of the time, "Revolution 9" was plainly an homage to electronic experimentalism. And had more audiences been aware of Stockhausen, the track might have done more to expand the audience for contemporary art music. But Stockhausen was (and remains today) a marginal figure to the general public, even though he was included in the album cover collage of *Sgt. Pepper's Lonely Hearts Club Band*. Without prior knowledge of Stockhausen, a listener would have only the sounds of "Revolution 9" to decipher, and these resist identification in a manner similar to that of musique concrète. "Revolution 9" was therefore ineffective as homage because the sounds Lennon strung together were too enigmatic, and the style too obscure, to communicate to any but a select few.

Musical appropriation as homage reached maturity with 1970s DJs who spun dance records and pop tunes at clubs and private parties in New York City during the 1970s. Using two turntables with a mixer and fader, a DJ could weave together whole songs or just break sections (i.e., when melody and vocals drop out, leaving only rhythm and percussion) of multiple songs into cohesive, extended works. Walter Gibbons, one of the earliest disco DJs, was famous for developing virtuosic "turntabling" moves such as quick cutting and simultaneous play of two records, techniques that would reappear in the nascent hip-hop movement of the mid-1970s.[11] While club DJs like Gibbons prided themselves on their encyclopedic mixes, early hip-hop DJs like Kool Herc appropriated the more exclusive canon of soul and funk. This selectivity was important for early black and Caribbean hip-hop audiences who soured at the commercialization of disco, and who gravitated toward more obscure black music associated with civil rights causes.[12]

Kool Herc's Afrocentric mixing style influenced later hip-hop tracks like Boogie Down Production's "South Bronx" (1986). The horn eruptions, guitar riffs, and nonverbal grunts of a James Brown song constitute the scaffolding for this celebration of Bronx hip-hop. DJ Scott La Rock intersperses Brown's exclamation, "Now that's what's happening!" throughout KRS-One's rapping on hip-hop history. Because of the strategic placement of this borrowing, the list of hip-hop trailblazers seems to impress Brown so much that he responds with his interjection, even though it was originally a reaction to his own music. For Boogie Down Production, the family tree of black pop begins with James Brown and continues through Afrika Bambaataa and Grandmaster Flash to their own music. Their rap *signifies* on James Brown's self-congratulatory yell, as if they gain respectability through association with the Godfather of Soul.

Signifyin' on previously created materials has appeared in various forms of African American art for at least the past two hundred years.[13] A signifyin' trope refers to, but does not quote verbatim from, older expressions. It instead adds ironic spin, sometimes contradicting the original meaning altogether. Signifyin' in music takes place when a song or style is imitated or repeated *with difference*, and has appeared in jazz, blues, disco, and rock 'n' roll.[14] When the hip-hop movement began in the Bronx in the mid-1970s, its earliest music consisted not of newly composed tracks but rather of cultural detritus: the break sections of old or obscure funk tracks by James Brown, the Isley Brothers, and other artists whose music resonated with young poor African Americans and Hispanics of

New York City. Identifying break beats became a sort of competition among club audiences, and DJs responded by choosing little-known tracks whose origins and significance would be known only to music connoisseurs. Some DJs obscured their cuts by adding noise in the form of "scratching," the noise produced when a record is pulled or pushed to play quickly forward or backward. As digital samplers began to replace turntables in hip-hop productions of the mid-1980s, DJs and producers further signified on their cuts by accelerating or slowing tempos and shifting pitches.

Dr. Dre's "Let Me Ride" (1992) presents a rich example of this musical revivalism through its juxtaposition of past and present. Dr. Dre defined the "gangsta" sound of West Coast hip-hop. His work with the group N.W.A (Niggas With Attitude) culminated with tracks like "Straight Outta Compton" and "Fuck Tha Police," songs that glorify misogyny, racially motivated violence, and urban rage. After N.W.A disbanded in 1991, Dre's solo projects led to *The Chronic*, an album pivotal not only for its crystallization of the gangsta musical aesthetic, but for its debut of rapper Snoop Doggy Dogg. *The Chronic* features the track "Let Me Ride," a manifesto of gangsta lifestyle replete with samples that signify on spirituals and funk. In "Let Me Ride," Dre portrays himself as a quintessential gangsta, a combination of neighborhood bully, pimp, and drug dealer. The gangsta figure is the present-day extension of the 1970s pimp, a black man who uses his wits, sex appeal, and brute force to negotiate a hostile world.[15] With this glamorous view of the 1970s in mind, however, one passage of "Let Me Ride" proves rather curious:

> No medallions, dreadlocks, or black fists
> It's just that gangsta glare, with gangsta raps[16]

Medallions, a symbol of the pimp decorated with gaudy gold chains; dreadlocks, the hairstyle of the Rastafarian; black fists, an icon of the

Black Power movement: Dre refuses all of these conventions. How can "Let Me Ride" be nostalgic for the 1970s if it rejects the political movements of that time?

While this lyric may disown 1970s radicalism, Dre repossesses the decade with his musical choices. "Let Me Ride" owes most of its musical material to Parliament's "Mothership Connection (Star Child)" (1975). "Mothership Connection" is itself a combination of original material with a quotation from an African American spiritual: "swing low, sweet chariot, stop and let me ride."[17] The alternation of Parliament's funk sound with the eerie modality of the spiritual creates a sort of musical reliquary in which remnants of the past are encased in modern form. The borrowings in "Let Me Ride" consist predominantly of synthesizer motives and a few sung choruses that are re-performed rather than sampled or scratched from "Mothership Connection." Dre uses the sampler to emulate the pops of vinyl and the reverse turntable scratches of a hip-hop DJ. So even though this track technically counts as re-performance (allusion) rather than sampling (duplication), the song was engineered to *sound* like duplication, something crucial to the aesthetics of hip-hop. The sounds of vinyl scratching reinforce the temporal distance separating the Parliament quotation from Dre's rapping. Despite the fact that the quote is a reproduction and not an "original," these digital additions are acoustic illusions, manufacturing a sense of authenticity or aura. In the final chorus of "Let Me Ride," the spiritual roots of the "Mothership Connection" are underscored by an even older recording of a man singing "Swing Low, Sweet Chariot." The result is a relic within a relic; Dre embeds an ancient phonographic recording within a sample from the funk era, juxtaposing slave songs and the sounds of the 1970s with those of today. The lyrics bring a sense of order to these musical juxtapositions, since Dre begins each chorus describing neighbors who greet him by singing the spiritual.

These acclamations suggest that Dre is the driver of the chariot. In spirituals, the chariot has long been a symbol of liberation and served as a code word for the Underground Railroad. The sacred imagery of the chariot in "Let Me Ride" is secularized even as Dre is likened to Moses. Sampling functions as a bridge linking the gangsta rapper to a 1970s funk band and an early-twentieth-century singer of spirituals.

As Tim Brennan writes, "rap tries to be . . . both the encyclopedia and the built-in commentary on all the African cultural production that existed before it."[18] Ice Cube's "The Product" (1990) is another rap track that questions civil-rights-era optimism through samples and collage techniques. Like Dr. Dre, Ice Cube was originally in the gangsta rap group N.W.A but left in 1990 to pursue a career as a solo rapper and film actor. "The Product" is a semi-autobiographical account of life in South Central Los Angeles. Cube describes the process through which a black man becomes a "product" of society. Uninterested in school, the teenager drops out to become a thief and gangbanger. He later decides to renounce crime in order to raise a family. But his past catches up with him, and he is sent to prison, where he contemplates suicide. Hopeless and nihilistic, "The Product" depicts an inner-city African American as the victim of parental and governmental neglect.

The samples in "The Product" are dense and more difficult to register than those in "Let Me Ride." They bombard the listener in quick succession, and although the rhythm creates a certain regularity, new sounds constantly emerge to provide audio commentary on Cube's lyrics. The text is divided into two large stanzas, separated by a refrain ("Yeah, yeah, yeah") and the words "Push a little harder," sampled from Sly and the Family Stone's "You Can Make It If You Try" (1969), which preaches the rewards of perseverance. Its inclusion in "The Product" is a sardonic commentary on the hopes of the 1960s. The federal programs designed to aid inner-city youth prove to be woefully inadequate, so no matter how hard he tries, the protagonist cannot just "make it."

The samples in "The Product" also signify on a past musical legacy. Sly and the Family Stone released a number of songs whose view of racial relations was constructive and optimistic (before they too succumbed to pessimism with their 1971 album *There's a Riot Goin' On*). The band was an integrated mix of races and genders, making it a utopian microcosm amid the turmoil of the late 1960s. Cube's verses are cynical, but a listener can choose to ignore them in order to pay attention to the music. The Sly/Stone sample achieves something more emotionally potent; like a funhouse mirror, sampling contorts the familiar into the grotesque.

In both "Let Me Ride" and "The Product," samples and borrowings from 1960s and 1970s songs become symbols of the era's naïveté. Reading these appropriations as signifyin' yields a rich assortment of possible interpretations and associations, but only for listeners who are already familiar with the older borrowings. For a listener who does not know the references, however, the context is potentially lost. Hip-hop audiences are aware of the function of sampling and turntabling as a means of conveying musical commentary that may support or contradict the message of the lyrics. And fans' eagerness to track down sampling sources has led to renewed interest in 1970s artists such as James Brown, Funkadelic and Parliament, and the Isley Brothers, and consequently has increased their album sales.[19] Until the late 1990s, when hip-hop DJs began to explore more esoteric sampling sources, most loops and sounds were taken from soul, funk, and disco of the 1970s. As a result, rap listeners have become accustomed to accepting a sample as an important soul work, even if they are not actually familiar with the song itself.

Soul music commands such respect that some producers create

new samples to imitate older soul. One such example is Lauryn Hill's "Doo Wop (That Thing)" (1998), which plays on the expectation that a sample will signify on older music, even though this particular song actually borrows no preexisting material. At the beginning of the track, Hill says, "Yo, remember back on the boogie when cats used to harmonize like 'ooh . . . ,'" at which point she and her female backup chorus sing an *a cappella* chord progression.[20] A loop of a piano playing two alternating chords commences, continuing through the course of the song. This *a cappella* moment disappears when the drumbeat enters, and Hill begins her rap warning men and women of the dangers of promiscuity. Two-thirds of the way through the track, the opening *a cappella* motive returns in a break section and the singers harmonize, as if inspired by Hill's reminiscence.

The title "Doo Wop" refers to the rhythm and blues form prevalent in the 1950s that featured four- or five-part *a cappella* harmony. Yet Hill's lyrics have nothing to do with doo wop. The song doesn't even borrow from any older material but instead loops the piano riff in a manner usually reserved for soul samples. If Hill had not situated her song within the past, the vocal interjections would not attract much notice. But because of the piano loop and Hill's evocation of black music history, "Doo Wop" intimates that it is sampling something "authentic." This authenticity is predicated on Hill's views of black identity. We need only turn to her ensuing lyrics criticizing black women who wear "hair weaves like Europeans" and "fake nails done by Koreans" to recognize Hill's agenda of prideful African American consciousness. By rejecting the existence of an authentic musical past, "Doo Wop" also questions the ideal of racial authenticity. The samples and Hill's lyrical allusion to older music create the expectation that we are hearing another homage to real soul music. This musical sleight-of-hand complements Hill's message, that many young blacks deceive themselves by creating fictive black identities. The effectiveness of this song hinges on the extent to which sampling successfully manufactures authenticity, or as Benjamin would describe it, aura.

Amiri Baraka has claimed that hip-hop sampling commodifies soul and strips it of meaning.[21] This observation is not particularly revelatory; DJs have long prided themselves on their systematic disassembly and reuse of soul. But while Baraka might complain that such commodification invalidates any claims hip-hop might have to authenticity, sampling has in fact become the favored means of creating the *illusion* of authenticity. As one further example shows, sampling sometimes obscures the racial identities of artists. The Tom Tom Club's "Genius of Love" (1981) is a quirky, synthesizer-laden track that has been sampled in several songs from Grandmaster Flash's "It's Nasty (Genius of Love)" to Mariah Carey's 1995 remake, "Fantasy." In fact, writes Jane Dark, "Genius of Love" "is so familiar, it's become just *one of those samples*, like 'Flashlight' or 'The Funky Drummer,' "[22] two hits by Parliament and James Brown, respectively. Unlike either P-Funk or James Brown's band, however, the Tom Tom Club was a joint project of Tina Weymouth and Chris Frantz, two whites who belonged to the New Wave group the Talking Heads. Concerning the Tom Tom Club and "Genius of Love," Dark continues: "calculating its contribution to future hip-hop, their one great song is a cultural treasure. And what *it* treasures is black sounds, calling out names of heroes like George Clinton and Bootsy Collins, and eventually just chanting 'James Brown, James Brown.' "[23] But "Genius of Love" is not a mere litany of soul names. Its synthesized idiosyncrasies signify on its forefathers, from the Bootsy Collins–like bass line to the stylized "James Brown" mantra that imitates the Godfather himself.

Just as "Genius of Love" honors black sounds, it is in turn cherished in subsequent borrowings. This white art-pop song becomes authentic enough to be considered black. Grandmaster Flash and the Furious Five (composed of five African American men) released what is probably the earliest sample of the track in a song titled "It's Nasty (Genius of Love)," also recorded in 1981. "It's Nasty" is a typical early hip-hop party track: the five MCs trade off bragging raps, while Grandmaster Flash, a DJ who popularized turntabling in hip-hop, spins a collage of funk beats. "It's Nasty" proceeds as follows: after a brief synthesized quotation of the opening to Aaron Copland's "Fanfare for the Common Man," the drumbeat, bass line, and synth melody of the Tom Tom Club track enter. After a few rhymes, Flash shifts to a bridge section with horns, music that does not come from "Genius of Love." Before returning to the Tom Tom Club sample, the five rappers shout, "Who needs a band when the beat just goes?" A provocative question, because the innovations of Grandmaster Flash and other DJs put the very necessity of using live musicians into question.

But this exclamation is more than just a reflection of the era's anxieties over technology; it signifies on the original text of "Genius of Love" as well. In the Tom Tom Club original, Tina Weymouth raps: "Stepping in rhythm to Kurtis Blow, who needs to think when your feet just go?"[24] Kurtis Blow was a key rapper in the early 1980s, so Weymouth's mentioning him demonstrates a knowledge of hip-hop that was certainly uncommon among whites at the time. The Furious Five signify on Weymouth's words because the Tom Tom Club already defined and valorized the elite of black musical creation. Who needs a band when the song can imitate James Brown and George Clinton? Who needs a band when sounds are at our fingertips? These are the questions that Flash asks us, but he has already answered them with his sonic collage. Flash need only re-suscitate the Tom Tom Club's homage to the Old School. While the Furious Five signify on the original text of "Genius of Love," no musical additions are necessary. Thanks to its catchy hooks and its praise of Old School greats, "Genius of Love" has transgressed the color barrier to join the black canon of soul samples. The devotion that subsequent black hip-hop acts have shown this song suggests that its treatment of Brown and P-Funk is more important than the actual identity of its performers. Indeed, "Genius of Love" is a perennial song on rap and R&B radio stations that otherwise play black artists exclusively.

Like their American cousins, hip-hop DJs from other countries often sample from the music of their own ethnic backgrounds as a way of signifyin' on their heritage. In Germany during the 1990s, Turkish hip-hop bands created a distinctly non-American approach to sampling. King Size Terror, a group from Nuremberg, rapped in Turkish and used typical hip-hop drum tracks adorned with snippets of Turkish ornamental arabesque music.[25] For audiences of Turkish descent, ancestral samples provide a sense of tradition that soul samples might lack. Sampling the materials of one's cultural heritage has become a common hip-hop device worldwide, such that DJs from India to Mexico intersperse local folk songs amid urban funk rhythms. In light of these practices, samples whose origins are identifiably different from those of the artist require explanation. From the 1970s to the mid-1990s, the majority of hip-hop samples and appropriations drew from soul and funk. But during this same period, other songs appropriated tunes that were unmistakably white and bore no relation to black culture. Run DMC's 1986 version of "Walk This Way" (originally recorded by Aerosmith) is the most famous example, but artists like Schooly D, A Tribe Called Quest, and the Geto Boys have also made use of country, heavy metal, and even singer-songwriter tracks. Crossover sampling facilitated rap's entrance into mainstream media. "Walk This Way," for instance, was the one of the first rap videos shown on MTV, and its success led to the launching of *Yo! MTV Raps*, a program devoted exclusively to hip-hop. The presence of an Aerosmith sample undoubtedly attracted listeners who might not otherwise have liked rap music, but more importantly, it won over MTV executives who were careful to present only rap songs that would not offend their largely white audience. As Ted Swedenberg explains, sampling white music transmits a political message as well:

> By placing such instantly recognizable rock riffs in the context of black music, rap artists "reinvent" them as black. They thereby assert African Americans' familiarity with, and claim to, the segregated rock heritage, while proclaiming the largely unacknowledged debt of that heritage to the work of black musicians.[26]

There is much to recommend this observation, but it explains 1980s hip-hop sampling better than that of the 1990s. During the premillennial era of "irrational exuberance," when stock market speculation contributed to a rise in the African American upper class, hip-hop began to broadcast images of urbane wealth and sophistication.[27] The street-hardened likes of Ice Cube and Tupac Shakur were suddenly rivaled by Puff Daddy, who displayed his vast riches with fashion, jewelry, and samples. "I'll Be Missing You" (1997) and "Come with Me" (1998), two of Puffy's most lucrative singles, sampled from white pop's aristocracy, Led Zeppelin and the Police. The licenses for these inclusions reportedly amounted to seven-figure sums. This is not to suggest that Puff Daddy chose samples solely on the basis of their price. Quite the contrary: he has repeatedly expressed his admiration for the materials he uses, but he also seems proud of the fact that he can afford to use them. In the late 1990s, sampling white music was really no longer about proving the legitimacy of hip-hop within a global market. Sampling had turned into a highly expensive operation, and "ghetto-fabulous" musicians sampled white music as a method of displaying financial wealth.

HIP-HOP COLLAGE, SAMPLING, AND THE LAW

The conspicuous consumption of Puff Daddy's sampling may be characteristic of the black *nouveau riche*, but it also reflects the economic realities of sampling and musical borrowing. According to current music industry practices, any musician who wants to reuse someone's recording has two choices: attempt to license the materials legally, or risk possible lawsuits by using the sounds without permission. Indicative of the sea change in hip-hop, Puff Daddy brags today about the samples he was able to clear, whereas in the late 1980s many rap artists bragged about the samples they stole. This environment has evolved as a result of legal confrontations stretching back to the early 1980s. Although music copyright infringement by no means originated with sampling, hip-hop *seemed* to introduce a new type of theft: the misappropriation of sound recordings. But unlike "The Flying Saucer" and other novelty records, much of early hip-hop aspired to be art or political commentary. Hip-hop has revolutionized global music production in a way that Dickie Goodman and his ilk never could have, and so judicial responses to hip-hop have understandably had a profound impact on the music industry at large.

The first legal conflict involving hip-hop appropriation concerned the Sugar Hill Gang's "Rapper's Delight," released in September 1979. The track was the first hip-hop song to gain exposure outside of the New York City area, scoring #4 on the Billboard R&B chart and #36 on the pop chart at its height. Producer Sylvia Robinson wanted to maximize the track's commercial appeal, so she structured "Rapper's Delight" on the model of Bronx hip-hop: a humorous rap set to a well-known funk or disco song. As accompaniment, Robinson chose "Good Times" by the disco-funk band Chic, a #1 hit on the pop chart earlier in May 1979. Hip-hop DJs at the time were still using turntables to mix songs manually; samplers were not used to make rap records until around 1983. Instead of hiring a DJ, however, Robinson had the Sugar Hill Records house band re-perform the instrument parts from "Good Times." Robinson's motivation may have been to make the song more radio-friendly, since few stations at the time were willing to play songs featuring the novel sound of turntable scratching.[28] Re-performance also allowed Sugar Hill Records to sidestep accusations of master recording theft. Nevertheless, Bernard Edwards and Nile Rodgers, the songwriting team for "Good Times," sued Sugar Hill Records for infringing on the composition copyright of their song. The two parties settled out of court before a verdict could be reached. The terms of the settlement included the awarding of full publishing credits for "Rapper's Delight" to Edwards and Rodgers.

Though the Sugar Hill case involves a sound-alike record—musical allusion rather than duplication—critics and listeners alike commonly assume that the lawsuit concerning "Rapper's Delight" was the first to involve digital sampling.[29] This would be a trivial error if we were simply considering musical aesthetics because after all, the Sugar Hill band was hired to imitate a sample. Moreover, most hip-hop from the late 1970s featured loops consisting of preexisting recordings rather than re-performances, so it's understandable that writers assume "Rapper's Delight" did the same. But this detail is critical in discussions concerning sampling lawsuits. Siva Vaidhyanathan describes "Rapper's Delight" as "spoken rhymes punctuating a background montage constructed from unauthorized pieces of previously recorded music."[30] He uses the Sugar Hill case as a starting point from which to frame the entire history of hip-hop sampling, a practice that he claims has been stunted by excessive lawsuits. Yet as we'll see below, re-performance cast as sampling is in no danger of disappearing; for many artists it is the only affordable and legal means of incorporating sample-like sounds. Had Sugar

Hill Records paid the statutory fee for licensing, "Rapper's Delight" would have been a judicial nonevent.

The first lawsuits involving *true* sampling started to appear in the mid-1980s. Jimmy Castor sued the Beastie Boys and Def Jam Records in 1986 for the use of a simple phrase, "Yo, Leroy," that originally appeared in Castor's "The Return of Leroy (Part I)." In 1989, the Turtles sued De La Soul for using a portion of their "You Send Me" track on Soul's *3 Feet High and Rising*. In 1990, David Bowie and Freddie Mercury sued Vanilla Ice for using the bass line and piano riffs of "Under Pressure" in Ice's groan-inducing "Ice Ice Baby."[31] These three cases were each settled out of court with the defendants agreeing to pay considerable sums in reparations. The first courtroom decision concerning sampling was reached in 1991 when Grand Upright Music sued Biz Markie, Warner Records, and Cold Chillin' Publishing for unauthorized sampling of Gilbert O'Sullivan's "Alone Again (Naturally)" (1972) in Biz Markie's "Alone Again" (1990) on the album *I Need a Haircut*.[32] Markie sang the three title words and used a lifted recording of O'Sullivan's piano accompaniment in a song that discussed Markie's difficulty in finding friends and romance.

Before his album was released, Markie attempted to contact O'Sullivan to obtain a sample clearance but received no response. Warner and Cold Chillin' assumed naively from this silence that no news was good news and released the album. The judge for this case condemned Markie's song as a direct violation not only of American copyright law, but of the Bible's Seventh Commandment disallowing theft. He even went so far as to recommend that the defendants be prosecuted for criminal copyright infringement, a more serious charge that carries its own fines and possibility of prison sentencing in addition to any damages awarded the plaintiff.[33] Before sentencing could be meted out, the parties settled for an undisclosed sum.[34]

But Markie's career suffered irreversible harm; the court ordered that
I Need a Haircut be removed from store shelves and radio playlists
until the album was reprinted without "Alone Again."[35]

For a few years after the Markie ruling, it seemed that unlicensed
sampling would be prosecuted categorically. In the 1993 Jarvis v.
A&M Records decision, a New Jersey District Court found that Se-
duction's sampling of Boyd Jarvis's "The Music's Got Me" (1982)
qualified as copyright infringement of both recording and composition, even though the borrowed materials consisted of only brief,
nonverbal exclamations.[36] In recent years, however, some courts have
argued that unlicensed sampling need not be considered an infringement if the borrowing work displays only "fragmented literal similarity" to its original.[37] For instance, Tuff 'n' Rumble Management lost
its lawsuit against Run DMC and Dana Dane for two reasons: the
plaintiffs could not prove they owned the copyrights for either the
recordings or the compositions, but more importantly, the sampled
drumbeats were recontextualized and changed significantly from
their source recording.[38] In 2001 Marley Marl sued Snoop Dogg for
sampling his "The Symphony," which itself had sampled from an
Otis Redding song, "Hard to Handle." Snoop attempted to have the
case dismissed by arguing that Marl could not claim copyright for
his composition because he himself infringed on Redding's recording to produce a derivative work. A New York District Court found
that Marl's recording was not substantially similar to the Redding
because it looped only two bars of the total song.[39] Therefore, Marl
could claim copyright protection over his own work and could file
suit against others who potentially infringed on it.

Similarly, in 2002 a District Court in California found that the
Beastie Boys' use of a three-note portion of James Newton's flute
piece "Choir" was not infringement because the borrowed notes
were not original enough to warrant copyright.[40] The Beastie Boys

had successfully negotiated with Newton's record label, ECM, in 1992 for rights to use the sound recording to "Choir," but did not acquire permission from Newton to sample the underlying composition. When Newton learned of the appropriation in 2000, he claimed that the passage (three flute multiphonics with added vocal interference) was original enough to count as protectable material.[41] Newton mounted a vigorous publicity campaign accusing the Beastie Boys of theft and the court of prejudice against African American forms of expressions.[42] But the Ninth Circuit Court of Appeals affirmed the District Court's findings, stating that even if the composition were sufficiently original to be protectable, the sample constituted a "de minimis" borrowing, meaning that it was too small to be recognizable.[43]

The Tuff 'n' Rumble, Marley Marl, and Newton decisions indicate that courts were willing to consider relationships between appropriating and appropriated works on a case-by-case basis. This trend was reversed with the 2004 decision of the Sixth Circuit Court of Appeals in *Bridgeport v. Dimension Films*, in which Bridgeport Music accused the rap group N.W.A of illegally sampling its recording of Funkadelic's "Get off Your Ass and Jam." A Tennessee District Court had previously ruled that the sample, comprised of a repeated, three-note electric guitar arpeggio, was a de minimis sample requiring no clearance.[44] The Sixth Circuit reversed this ruling, declaring:

A sound recording owner has the exclusive right to "sample" his own recording. [. . .] Get a license or do not sample. We do not see this as stifling creativity in any significant way. It must be remembered that if an artist wants to incorporate a "riff" from another work in his or her recording, he is free to [re-perform] the sound of that "riff" in the studio [. . .] [T]he market will control the license price and keep it within bounds. The sound recording copyright holder cannot exact

a license fee greater than what it would cost the person seeking the
license to just [re-perform] the sample in the course of making the
new recording.[45]

This verdict mistakenly assumes that the compulsory license for song
covers exerts any influence on licensing fees for master recordings.
As Puff Daddy's sampling has demonstrated, licenses are negotiated, and nothing prevents a sound recording owner from setting an
astronomical price for a sample. This ruling also retreats from previous courts' nuanced readings of samples by refusing to consider
how much a sample has been changed or recontextualized. Unless
other judges radically critique the *Bridgeport v. Dimension* decision,
this verdict will probably force sampling to remain a pay-per-use
technique in commercially released music.

Before Biz Markie's well-publicized legal battle, some rap artists
glamorized illegal sampling in their lyrics. Public Enemy's "Caught,
Can I Get a Witness?" (1988) is an often-discussed example of the
outrage some musicians felt at the increasing pressure to abandon
sampling.[46] Chuck D's lyrics frame the conflict racially, with white-
run record companies and "Uncle Tom" black musicians ganging up
against hip-hop. Ice Cube's "Jackin' for Beats" (1990) explores the
materiality of samples, submerging the listener in a kaleidoscopic
array of song fragments. His lyrics compare sampling to "jackin'," or
stealing. But for Ice Cube, theft is a means of homage: accompanied
by part of a Public Enemy song (a group Cube openly admires), Cube
raps, "and even if they're down with my crew, I'll jack them too."[47]
Such reveling in the lawlessness of sampling has since fallen out
of fashion, at least among artists of Ice Cube's rank. The 1991 Biz
Markie decision undoubtedly frightened the hip-hop community,
but to claim, as Vaidhyanathan has, that "[r]ap music since 1991

has been marked by a severe decrease in the amount of sampling" is to oversimplify a complicated situation.[48] The Markie decision was a bold recognition of the proprietary nature of sound recordings, and initially, it scared record labels into insisting on clearances before sampling. But the Markie decision was also a boon for record labels because it effectively allowed recording copyright owners free rein over pricing.

The true ramifications of the Markie case are more insidious. Prior to 1991, sampling was a practice that ran the gamut of the hip-hop world, from obscure and independent artists to the biggest names, with moderately successful Biz Markie in the middle. After 1991, sampling persisted among artists on the extremes: those who were either rich enough to afford licensing or obscure enough to be able to risk illegal sampling. Well-off artists like Puff Daddy might be able to afford one blockbuster sample per song, but not any others, so that one sample would be looped repeatedly (as in the case of "I'll Be Missing You"). But the middle ground occupied by smaller major-label and independent artists witnessed the greatest change as re-performance replaced sampling (as in "Rapper's Delight"). Some artists abandoned borrowing altogether, opting for studio-created, original sounds.

Not coincidentally, sampling choices in post-Markie hip-hop expanded to include not only funk and soul but virtually any form of recorded music. This broadening of the musical palette was due in part to the avoidance of licensing and lawsuits. A musician is less likely to be sued if he samples something unknown because few listeners would even know that the material was unoriginal. And like the earliest disco DJs who searched for arcane records to spin, today's artists choose their samples in such a way as to demonstrate their command over diverse musical cultures and traditions.

SAMPLADELIA AND THE FOREIGN

Turntablism and sampling have been controversial practices in hip-hop, but this does not mean that sampling occurs *only* in hip-hop. Turntable scratching first emerged in late-1960s New York and Miami dance club music, which by the 1970s was known as disco. Even after disco "died" in the early 1980s, disco DJing techniques thrived in the underground house music scenes of Chicago, New York, and London. House DJs replaced their disco records with soul, synth-pop, and salsa. As digital samplers began to permeate the market in the 1980s, house music in Detroit metamorphosed into techno, a catchall term for electronic dance music featuring futuristic, mechanized beats and generally nonreferential samples.[49] In other words, sampling has been a defining characteristic not only of hip-hop, but also of dance music as a whole since the 1970s, so much so that Simon Reynolds refers to the myriad forms of sample-based hip-hop and electronic dance music as "sampladelia."[50]

The entrance of digital samplers changed music production fundamentally by enabling the appropriation of any imaginable sound. Although *sampladelia* is a broad term pertaining to a variety of styles, many works of sampladelia reflect a fascination with sounds deliberately drawn from outside of pop audiences' orbits. This co-optation of "foreign" music (whether foreign in terms of geography, ethnicity, gender, or era) can be a politically charged gesture because it puts into relief questions of power and identity. Artists who sample the foreign demonstrate their knowledge of, and often dominance over, other traditions. To examine contemporary foreign appropriations, we must turn to analyses of earlier musical traditions in which appropriation was equally prevalent.

The theorist Kofi Agawu has characterized the use of different styles and genres in music of the Classical period (i.e., European concert music dating from ca. 1750 to 1810) as an interplay of "topics." To abbreviate Agawu's definition, topics are musical signs, meaning they function through the interaction of a *signifier* and a *signified*. The term signifier in a topic corresponds to its raw musical characteristics: rhythm, meter, tempo, pitch, harmony, and so on. The signified in a topic is indicated by "conventional labels drawn mostly from eighteenth-century historiography (Sturm und Drang, fanfare, learned style, sensibility, and so on)."[51] Agawu finds topical analysis of great value when considering certain works by Haydn, Mozart, and Beethoven because it allows us to categorize different types of music rather than having to treat every particular passage as unique. But he rightfully critiques this method for not explaining the syntax of classical music. For while we might correctly identify a succession of topics in a certain passage, this type of analysis cannot explain why one topic follows another. Nor does it address the large-scale patterns of rhetoric that infuse classical music, like the fact that many classical works operate according to highly structured and ritualized forms.

While Agawu goes on to fashion a form of analysis that he believes best suits classical music, popular music studies require a different approach. In sampladelia, song form is mostly idiosyncratic, so there are few general rules dictating harmony, section breaks, or texture. To put it another way, there are no syntactical guidelines indicating *how* one sample follows another or which samples should be used. Thus topical analysis, handicapped by its inability to account for large-scale form, seems to be well suited to sampladelia, where small-scale change is of paramount importance.

Since the 1980s, interest in non-Western music has increased thanks to a shift in favor of such liberal concepts as diversity and multiculturalism. First World artists such as Peter Gabriel, Paul Simon, and Sting have embraced world music by collaborating with non-Western musicians. Perhaps the most famous example of this is Paul Simon's 1986 *Graceland* album, which utilizes South African and Latino musicians.[52] The politics of such cross-cultural collaboration constitute an ethical minefield. Writers such as Steven Feld, Charles Hamm, and George Lipsitz have evaluated such exchanges by the degree to which First World artists compensate their collaborators.[53] According to this reasoning, successful "royalty artists" (meaning the musicians who headline a project) have a moral responsibility to share credits and sales with any studio musicians they hire. In the case of Paul Simon, who paid his partners and often listed them as co-composers, critics have nonetheless faulted him for appropriating African sounds as musical curiosities. After *Graceland* was completed, Simon could resume his enviable status in America, while the group that collaborated with Simon, Ladysmith Black Mambazo, had to return to apartheid South Africa.

In the cases described above, non-Western musicians *agreed* to work for First World artists. Since the early 1990s, however, interest in global sounds has taken an even more controversial tack.[54] Several European and American pop artists have sampled non-Western sounds without permission, creating a blizzard of highly publicized court cases but little in the way of legal precedent. One common cross-cultural sampling scenario involves an ethnographical recording that is "discovered" by First World pop talent. For example, an ethnomusicologist records traditional music that is then released on a label dedicated to the preservation of native cultures, such as UNESCO or Maison des Cultures du Monde.[55] The copyright of this master recording is owned neither by the musicians nor by the ethnographer, but by the record label. A First World artist who decides to use the field recording arranges licensing with the record label but consults neither the ethnomusicologist nor the musicians. These cases are ethically problematic, yet often, no laws get broken

in such scenarios. Many non-Western field recordings feature traditional music that has no authorial attribution. Such pieces are
usually considered to have "anonymous" authorship, meaning either that they reside in the public domain or that a copyright has
been assigned to the compiler rather than to the performer. Because
of this legal loophole, First World artists like Enigma maintain that
they have conducted themselves legally and ethically.

In 1993, the German-based New Age group Enigma released "Return to Innocence," a multimillion-dollar hit that uses a field recording of two aboriginal Taiwanese singers. "Return to Innocence" was
in heavy rotation on radio stations worldwide and was used in a promotional video for the 1996 Olympic Games in Atlanta.[56] Despite
this exposure, the singers who performed the Enigma refrain never
received any payment for the borrowing, nor was their permission
even sought for the track. In 1997 they filed suit against Enigma
artist Michael Cretu and his representing companies, Virgin Records
and EMI, for unauthorized use of the material. As with most sampling litigation, this case was settled out of court for an undisclosed
sum of money and attribution of the singers on all future printings
of the single.

Sampled non-Western music has appeared in modern pop because to many First World audiences, such music sounds fresh, authentic, and sincere. Given their unfamiliar languages and musical
idioms, foreign samples translate into a general topic of exoticness,
a blank slate onto which audiences can impose romantic fantasies.
American hip-hop DJs during the late 1990s and the early years
of the twenty-first century, for instance, turned to Indian music
for exotic samples.[57] The most famous legal showdown resulting
from this practice involved a West Coast DJ's sampling of a Bappi
Lahiri song from the soundtrack for the Bollywood film *Jyoti*.[58] The
Lahiri composition was reused in a song called "Addictive," which

was performed by R&B artist Truth Hurts. Three months after its release in July 2002, "Addictive" sold six hundred thousand copies and made it to the Top 10 Billboard rap chart. Lahiri won a preliminary victory in February 2003 when he was granted an injunction preventing future sales of "Addictive" until the song's liner notes were changed to credit him as a co-composer. Lahiri also threatened to sue for compensatory damages in excess of $1 million for his loss of potential sales in the United States. Saregama, the film production company that owns the copyright to *Jyoti*'s soundtrack, sued Dr. Dre (executive producer for Truth Hurts), Interscope, and Universal for an astronomical $500 million for copyright infringement of the master recording of *Jyoti*. Predictably, these cases settled out of court for undisclosed sums of money.

DJ Quik produced "Addictive" and chose the Lahiri sample. As Quik recounts, his discovery of the Lahiri soundtrack occurred by chance:

> I woke up one morning, [. . .] I turned on the TV and landed on this Hindi channel and just turned it up real loud [. . .]. There was a commercial on, and I just got up and went into the bathroom and started brushing my teeth. [. . .] Before I knew it, I was grooving. [. . .] [The beat] was just in my body. I went back in there and looked at the TV—there was a girl on there belly dancing, just like real fly. So I pushed record on the VCR. [59]

DJ Quik discovered the perfect orientalist artifact: a catchy groove with sexuality implicit in its sound. Unlike the "Return to Innocence" case, however, the "Addictive" situation is ethically murkier. Bappi Lahiri is one of India's most prolific "Bollywood" film composers and is among the most handsomely paid musicians worldwide. Lahiri has himself used unauthorized appropriations of American popular music in his dance numbers. Perhaps in response to the exposure of this case, in 2003 Lahiri released *Bappiwood Remixes*, an album of remixes of his own work including the very song involved in this lawsuit. The cover to *Bappiwood Remixes* (fig. 1) shows Lahiri co-opting Western showbiz trappings such as tacky sunglasses, the microphone of a pop singer, and the lettering of the famous Hollywood sign. Hardly a victim of Western appropriation, Bappi Lahiri is adept both at remixing and at using IP laws to protect his work.

Because the Lahiri sample DJ Quik used was copyrighted as a master recording, its legal status as protectable intellectual property is nearly irrefutable. So why did Interscope even try using this sample in the first place? Funk and soul samples cost top dollar, so hip-hop producers see Third World music as an untapped cache of cheap, crowd-pleasing sounds. Foreign music also seems a safer choice for unauthorized usage because often the copyrights are owned by obscure or even defunct companies. Especially in the case of ethnomusicological field recordings, the chances that an illegal sample would be caught later are considerably smaller than if American or European music were used. In short, the cost of licensing has led to shifts in sampling choices.

It is not enough to stop here with what is an obvious conclusion: non-Western samples function in a traditionally exoticist manner, invoking sensual, naive cultures. But it's important to start with works as simplistic as these in order to make a few general observations. First, DJs sample exotic sounds to demonstrate their own aesthetic reach, to prove how eclectic their tastes are. Second, copyright and licensing fees partially explain why world music has become the latest fashion in sampling. Although each of the cases mentioned here has led to some sort of legal showdown, the majority of cross-cultural appropriations pass unchallenged. In an environment where pop samples are expensive and unauthorized sampling invites trouble, sampling the foreign is both faddish and legally more secure.

Figure 1. Bappi Lahiri takes on Hollywood
(courtesy of Quicksilver Records).

Hip-hop sampling lawsuits first originated in the United States as an attempt to protect the interests of copyright owners and artists. But unfortunately, the glut of lawsuits around 1991 led to the creation of an arbitrary, expensive licensing system and a favorable climate for producers and DJs to turn to foreign samples as an affordable, safe alternative.

A second strand of collage music samples from a different type of exotic, the avant-garde of the twentieth and twenty-first centuries. The avant-garde does not purport to communicate to the masses, and thus in a fundamental way opposes the premises of popular music. The following two examples are challenging to decipher because they contain no lyrics that would aid with interpretation. Yet these two songs also contain the same elements listed above: they use the topic of the avant-garde to show off the DJ's aesthetic breadth, and they engage on some level with samples and their status as intellectual property.

DJ Spooky (Paul Miller) has been active since the mid-1990s. His music is difficult to categorize because of his eclectic sampling choices. His stage name obviously draws from club and rap disk jockeys who also go by the title "DJ." And DJ Spooky does make music that often sounds like hip-hop, with African American rhythm patterns and grooves. Yet he incorporates synthesized sounds, non-Western, obscure regional music, and the avant-garde into his mixes. One of his most famous collaborations was a 1996 concert tour with the New York new music ensemble ST-X and Iannis Xenakis. DJ Spooky is also a prolific writer who theorizes about sampling and music aesthetics. His texts are themselves collages, liberally mixing academic fixtures like Plato and Theodor Adorno with references to pop culture subjects such as *The Matrix* film franchise. Spooky describes his theory on the perception of musical collage as follows:

It's the structure of the perceptions and the texts and the memories that are conditioned by your thought-process that will echo and configure the way that texts you're familiar with rise into prominence when you think. We live in an era where quotation and sampling operate on such a deep level that the archaeology of what can be called knowledge floats in a murky realm between the real and unreal.[60]

In other words, our individual experiences as listeners determine our reactions to a piece: what we find familiar, and what we don't. This language echoes Pierre Henry, who based his work on the juxtaposition of collected and synthesized sounds. DJ Spooky calls attention to the slippage between the familiar and the unfamiliar in tracks like "Anansi Abstrakt" (1996), which samples the first measure of Claude Debussy's "Syrinx." To those familiar with twentieth-century music, "Syrinx" is a staple of modernism, a steppingstone for future avant-garde flute works by Varèse, Luciano Berio, and Brian Ferneyhough. Ultimately, whether or not a listener knows "Syrinx" doesn't matter, however, because the sample undergoes a two-part process of alienation: it is transposed down several half steps and then looped. After a few repetitions, even those accustomed to "Syrinx" may no longer think of it as familiar—it becomes dislodged from its context, an empty signifier. Then, in a manner identical to that of hip-hop, a groove fades in, and suddenly the Debussy seems to "fit" with its surroundings, even though "Syrinx" is in a triple meter and the percussion section in "Anansi Abstrakt" plays in a duple meter. This groove, a standard hip-hop percussion pattern emphasizing the downbeat while syncopating the other beats of the measure, forces "Syrinx" into a familiar context. This groove fades in and out throughout the track, intermittently exposing the "Syrinx" fragment.

The familiar and foreign collide in "Anansi Abstrakt," and DJ

Spooky orchestrates this meeting masterfully with his knowledge of pop conventions. In hip-hop or electronica, classical concert music stands out because of its harmony, timbre, and instrumentation, so it sounds foreign whether or not the listener actually knows the piece. A common feature of much sampladelia is the groove, a repetition or looping usually played by bass or percussion instruments. DJ Spooky introduces a deliberately foreign borrowing, forcefully integrates it into the familiar, and then rips it away from that foundation. At stake here is not DJ Spooky's definition of foreignness, nor, for that matter, our own. What is important is the process by which a listener reconciles sounds that do not seem to fit well together, and more fundamentally, how definitions of the familiar and exotic can change over time.

John Wall is a British collage composer who draws heavily from recent avant-garde music. His piece "Construction I" combines studio improvisations with samples from works by Richard Barrett, Harrison Birtwistle, Mauricio Kagel, and Iannis Xenakis. This recording sounds like a CD played in fast-forward. The samples are minuscule and virtually too fast to be identified. Wall is exploring the very definition of unfamiliarity. He chooses some of the most obscure recorded music available and dismembers it to the point of sheer unintelligibility. And yet there is a sort of groove even here, a rhythmic looping of various liminal sounds such as the extreme low and high registers or extreme speed. Even his album cover for *Constructions* is hard to read: pressed on a blank white envelope, the title is printed with embossed letters, but there is no ink, making it difficult to read and impossible to reprint in this book. Wall has said that his "main concern has always been to try and produce a coherent collage of music, sound, [and] noise that has some emotional and formal complexity to it."[61] He assembles meaningless parts into larger fragments of sound that barely possess familiar musical trappings such as a regular beat, creating music that sounds at once familiar and almost aggressively strange.

Both DJ Spooky and John Wall have stated in interviews that they are aware of the precarious legal position in which sampling places them.[62] DJ Spooky aligns himself with figures such as Lawrence Lessig who champion the "commons," a site of communally held cultural and intellectual property. For Spooky, sampling is a conceptual means of engaging with political issues. John Wall does not feel that his music is anti-copyright, and he disavows any political agenda regarding sampling. And because his samples are so difficult to identify, he sidesteps the copyright issue altogether. Yet Wall knows as well as DJ Spooky that his profile as a relatively obscure, independent-label composer renders him largely immune to lawsuits. The type of music Wall samples makes relatively little money anyway, so the perceived threat of litigation is much lower than if he were sampling popular music. In other words, the mere fact that their samples are exotic grants DJ Spooky and Wall freedom they might not otherwise enjoy if they chose more familiar collage materials.

Musical collage is frequently classified as postmodern, although many still debate what precisely constitutes musical postmodernism. Writers like David Harvey, Fredric Jameson, and Lawrence Kramer have stated that citation, pastiche, and collage characterize a postmodernist approach to music.[63] But a drawback of postmodernist theory is that it fails to address what citation implies. We can agree that sampladelia borrows from disparate sources, but how do we explain the fact that different listeners may react to samples differently? Is there any way to talk objectively about musical meaning in a work where citation leads to many different possible interpretations?

The disparate pieces examined in this chapter represent trends that provide a point of departure for analysis. Many collage materials are chosen not only for their meaning, but also for their economic value. Licensing certain types of music is more expensive than licensing others. Obscure music is attractive because it can often be obtained cheaply. So we can dispose with the romantic myth that all compositional choices are made because a composer is free to make them. Second, many of the pieces discussed here use music that is foreign or liminal. Topical analysis of such pieces proves very valuable because it acknowledges different types of music without necessarily emphasizing their exact origins. And this is crucial, because many collage pieces elicit a listening experience that is geared less toward precise identification of sources than toward a juxtaposition of *types* of music. The motivations of the artists are useful in deciphering music, but they cannot give us the whole picture. A composer need not be completely aware of every subtle implication of a sample used. Indeed, a listener's experience of a piece may be totally different from the one intended by the composer, as the musique concrète polemic demonstrated.

Allusion and duplication are becoming indistinguishable in the wake of new advances in software technology. Programs like Pro Tools allow users to undertake sophisticated recording, editing, and mixing work on home computers. These programs are, in effect, the word processors of the recording industry and are affordable on an amateur's budget. With enough expertise, a user of Pro Tools can alter recorded data to the point that it sounds entirely different from its origins; likewise, this technology can create sounds that seem identical to preexisting materials. In other words, distinguishing between an exact reproduction and a mere allusion is becoming increasingly difficult. In the early 1990s, it was still possible for courts to detect sampling because analog methods of mixing required that a sample have the same tempo as the original source.[64] If the tempo had been slowed down, the key or pitch of the melody would be correspondingly lower, in the same way that a record played at a slow speed will sound lower in pitch than when it is played at normal speed.

Today, programs like Pro Tools allow for the manipulation of pitch and tempo independently, enabling the user to add or subtract sounds with the precision of a surgeon's scalpel. Determining (ontologically or legally) where a sample stops and a new composition begins has become nearly impossible. Given this challenge, we would do well to recall the musique concrète debate concerning residual signification. Schaeffer urged listeners to read all sounds as abstractions, divorced from their origins. Henry embraced the past associations of his borrowings, but used these found objects to compose original pieces. Judges and legislators might follow Henry's lead in considering the legitimacy of transformative appropriation. The origins of samples might very well be less important than the ways in which sampladelia artists use them to create new works.

CHAPTER FOUR

The Shadow of the Law

The narrator of W. G. Sebald's *Austerlitz* (2001) portrays the monstrous, recently built Bibliothèque Nationale as an edifice whose architecture discourages, if not renders impossible, the free flow of knowledge: "we began a long, whispered conversation in the *Haut-de-jardin* reading room, which was gradually emptying now, about the dissolution, in line with the inexorable spread of processed data, of our capacity to remember, and about the collapse, *l'effondrement* [. . .] of the Bibliothèque Nationale which is already under way. The new library building, which in both its entire layout and its near-ludicrous internal regulation seeks to exclude the reader as a potential enemy, might be described [. . .] as the official manifestation of the increasingly importunate urge to break with everything which still has some living connection to the past."[1] Sebald's depiction of the French national library is analogous to the state of IP law today because recent applications of copyright and trademark laws have similarly stifled the free exchange of cultural production that, at least until recently, was supposed to characterize thriving civilizations. Lawrence Lessig has likened the situation to a "land grab," whereby media and entertainment corporations acquire and defend cultural products in order to charge fees for their use and appropriation.[2]

McLeod, Coombe, Lessig, Vaidhyanathan, as well as other media scholars, cultural theorists, journalists, activists, and lawyers are outraged at the intrusion of IP law into everyday life. They decry exorbitant licensing fees, increasing copyright protection terms, and lawsuits undertaken to intimidate creators into abandoning their projects. These writers have triggered a large-scale reconsideration of the purpose of IP law, which they hope will result in legislation that balances the interests of publishers, record labels, film studios, and media corporations with those of authors, artists, and consumers. But as Rosemary Coombe has observed, IP law simultaneously threatens and catalyzes cultural production.[3] Music is not a passive victim at the hands of Time Warner or the Supreme Court. Many composers and musicians challenge the encroachments of IP law directly through activism as well as through innovative forms of musical appropriation. Some of these activities are legal, while others are flagrantly illegal. These gestures of rebellion are affecting the music industry's business models. IP law enforcement is intended to prevent plagiarism and piracy, but despite itself, it emboldens artists to develop methods of appropriation that actually enrich musical discourse. This observation is not meant to condone laws such as the Copyright Term Extension Act, nor to absolve corporate bodies that initiate specious lawsuits in order to scare musicians away from sampling or borrowing. Rather, key examples of musical appropriation and consequent litigation demonstrate that excessive IP protections are harmful not only to creators, but ultimately to the entertainment industry as a whole.

The four major record label distributors (EMI, Sony-BMG, Universal, and Warner) are scrambling to devise new production strategies that cater to consumer preferences for Internet downloading rather than traditional record store purchases. Similar models are being applied to methods of musical appropriation that in the past were expensive and difficult to license through major labels. Meanwhile, a vast array of underground and independent methods of appropriation is allowing many musicians to sidestep the majors altogether. Following the laws of supply and demand, the value of the major labels' protected property will decrease in value as more independent artists make their material available for little or no cost. This change may take some years to occur, but the fact remains that presently it is easy and cheap to reproduce many musical materials legally. And the record industry is coming to realize that it must reduce the price of sampling in order to remain competitive.

IP litigation occurs only when there is enough money at stake to warrant filing a lawsuit, which means that defendants in most IP infringement cases are financially solvent and well known. Most collage artists escape litigation altogether because their output generates little or no profit. Nanette Simon, a former Disney Corporation attorney, described the process through which content providers assess potential copyright claims as follows:

> They have attorneys on staff who make a determination as to whether they would even have a claim . . . and then they make a real-world determination of "Are we going to make any money? Is anybody going to see this? Do we really care?" If they do care, and some care more than others [. . .], they write a letter and they say "Stop." They say, "Use your original [materials], or don't do it at all."[4]

Simon may seem to be stating the obvious, but cultural critics thus far have depicted IP law as categorically harmful, such that any musician who borrows material (no matter how obscure or marginal) risks the type of lawsuit that destroyed Biz Markie's career. This is an understandable misrepresentation, but a misrepresentation nonetheless. We are preoccupied with major label artists because they usually receive the most media attention. But studying the effects of IP law on music by looking only at major label talent is to ignore the vast majority of musicians who do not appropriate from famous artists or who exploit loopholes in copyright law to their artistic and financial advantage.

IT TAKES A NATION OF LAWYERS TO HOLD US BACK

One can see why IP law has a bad reputation. Since the early 1990s, a number of writers have documented how creativity suffers at the hands of corporations that profit by exploiting copyright and trademark laws.[5] This exploitation seldom escalates beyond forms of intimidation known as "cease-and-desist" letters that threaten legal action if a work is not removed from circulation. Most publishing and recording contracts charge musicians with securing licensing for any borrowed materials, which means that the artist, not the label, is liable in the event of an infringement case.[6] When faced with a cease-and-desist letter, the average musician capitulates rather than paying exorbitant lawyers' fees to fight the lawsuit.

Unfortunately, abiding by the law can sometimes be just as expensive. As one of the most effective forms of musical allusion, 1950s cover songs enabled rock 'n' roll to transcend racial and ethnic boundaries. Recorded rock 'n' roll covers also precipitated the shift from a score-based to a recording-based music industry. Record labels produced covers cheaply and quickly thanks to the compulsory mechanical license. This statutory license has increased from its original 2.0 cents per song in 1909 to the 2004–5 rates of 8.5 cents per unit for a song lasting five minutes or less and 1.65 cents per minute for a song over five minutes.[7] Today, however, most record labels negotiate lower quarterly mechanical licenses with publishers rather than pay monthly royalties stipulated by law. These negotiated licenses, usually 75 percent of the statutory rate, are known as the "3/4's mechanical rate."[8] Publishers pass this reduction on to their talent by writing in the three-quarters mechanical license as a condition for signing, meaning that artists are forced to accept a 25 percent cut in royalties each time their compositions are covered. Artists who perform covers are usually required to sign contracts stating that their label will license only up to twice the reduced three-quarters rate for singles. Any royalties exceeding this amount must be paid by the recording artist, not by the label.[9] Musicians with modest financial means are unable to record more than one or two cover songs per album because their record companies won't pay for the licensing. In addition, there are few financial incentives for artists to record cover versions rather than their own material. When a cover version is performed over the radio, only the publishers and author of the original song, and not the performers themselves, receive performance royalties.

Live performances of cover songs have become equally problematic in recent years. An entertainer who sings someone else's material in concert is responsible for paying a negotiable performance royalty unless the venue owner pays for licensing. These royalties are almost always paid out to performance rights organizations like ASCAP or BMI, which share proceeds with publishers. The publishers in turn split royalties with the original songwriters. The music industry developed this system to ensure that songwriters and publishers be compensated for public performances and broadcasts. But how far should this royalty rule extend? Many musicians get their start by playing for modest or no compensation in bars, restaurants, and cafés. Not all of these venues pay performance rights royalties. Should the musician always be forced to pay a royalty if the venue does not? Musicians who play for ticket-buying crowds conceivably have a responsibility to pay the royalty, but what about those who play for free at the open-mike night of their local coffeehouse?

The law does not distinguish between what we might call "formal" musical events (where a professional plays for payment) and "informal" events, where music making occurs spontaneously and without monetary compensation. Publishers and performance rights organizations are amending the definition of formal events to include music making once considered below the legal radar. In 1996 ASCAP threatened several children's summer camps with lawsuits unless they stopped "public performances" (i.e., singing around a campfire) of "This Land Is Your Land" and "Ring Around the Rosie."[10] In 2000 a lawyer demanded that patrons of a Manhattan bar stop their sing-alongs unless they paid performance royalties.[11] Are these threats justified? No. Could these cases have been successfully litigated? Perhaps, but the question is usually moot. When faced with a cease-and-desist letter, many organizations and musicians choose to cave in, in the same way that some business owners pay "protection money" to the mob. But that having been said, are we at the point where children can no longer sing "Happy Birthday to You" at parties without Summy-Birchard Music, a subsidiary of Time Warner, suing for damages? It depends on where the party is held. It's unrealistic to claim that music publishers can monitor every use of their content, but more to the point, they care only about instances from which they could profit. We may well have arrived at the point where Olive Garden waiters must serenade customers with the chain's own faux-Italian birthday song because restaurant performances of "Happy Birthday to You" are actionable. But the bad press and public backlash produced by such excessive enforcement may prove an equally potent deterrent for litigious content providers.[12]

Even with the twofold licensing that most digital samples require, most artists who enter into recording contracts are personally responsible for obtaining and paying for permissions for using master recordings and compositions. Clearing samples is often a

time-consuming and confusing process, especially for those unfamiliar with the music industry. For this reason, "sampling clearance
houses" provide the service of negotiating and obtaining permissions
to reproduce samples. Diamond Time is one of the foremost copyright clearance companies in the United States, licensing samples
for artists represented by both major record labels and independents.
The publishing and recording rights are two separate clearances, and
the total cost for one sample clearance process is at least $900.[13] But
even when an artist can afford to purchase sampling rights, Diamond
Time does not guarantee a clearance agreement. Some artists and
labels are fundamentally resistant to the borrowing of their work and
will not grant permission at any price. Biz Markie learned this the
hard way with Gilbert O'Sullivan; other sample-resistant catalogs
include the works of Anita Baker, the Beatles, and Prince.[14] Record
companies like Polygram Label Group require that lyric sheets be
submitted with the clearance proposal and reserve the right to reject
the submission if they deem the new song to be unflattering to the
original artist.

As mentioned before, the composition license for a mechanical
reproduction per unit (single copy of the recording) was set for 2004–
5 at 8.5 cents for a song lasting five minutes or less or 1.65 cents per
minute for a song over five minutes. But in many songs featuring
sampling, the artist and publisher negotiate an alternative royalty
fee in which composition credits are shared, because the sample may
comprise only a small portion of either the original or the new song.
In 1998 the cheapest publishing clearance fees for a "2/4 bar use"
started with a $2,000 advance and up to 50 percent of the new song's
publishing credits, meaning that the artist and publisher of the new
song would have to share half of the songwriting proceeds with the
publisher of the borrowed song.[15] Sound recording copyrights have
no statutory rate, so labels enjoy complete freedom to determine

their prices. According to industry insiders, the minimum cost for master recording clearances currently hovers between $2,000 and $7,000 plus $0.02–$0.04 for every unit sold (to ensure both a minimum of compensation for songs that do not sell, as well as graduated income for commercially successful tracks).[16] If a sound belongs to a high-profile musician or company, the fees would naturally be much higher. Puff Daddy offered 50 percent of the proceeds for his 1997 hit "I'll Be Missing You" to the publishers of the Police's "Every Breath You Take." Because of the high sales of this track, the Police undoubtedly received several million dollars in compensation.[17]

FAIR USE AND THE COPY LEFT

Journalists and musicians alike regard Public Enemy's 1988 album *It Takes a Nation of Millions to Hold Us Back* as a paragon of compositional freedom. A *Nation of Millions* remains relevant in popular culture university courses and critical discussions of hip-hop. Its longevity stems not only from its politicized lyrics but also from its well-crafted juxtapositions of words and music. Sample-laden tracks bombard the listener with dizzying arrays of citations, including recordings of Black Power rallies and Isaac Hayes, James Brown and Anthrax. The opening of "Bring the Noise" teasingly repeats Malcolm X saying, "Too black, too strong." "Show 'Em Whatcha Got" uses a John Coltrane melody in tandem with a sampled speech praising activists such as Marcus Garvey and Nelson Mandela. Chuck D's lyrics urge a return to civil-rights-era ideals, but they also recount the band's confrontations with record companies looking to block their use of samples.

When Def Jam Records first released A *Nation of Millions*, most hip-hop samples were not licensed at all. To release just one of the songs from A *Nation of Millions* today, Public Enemy would have to pay advance licensing fees exceeding half of the amount the group expected to earn from sales of the entire album.[18] According to Siva Vaidhyanathan, transformative appropriation as exemplified by Public Enemy has been rendered all but impossible because of licensing fees: "The death of tricky, playful, transgressive sampling occurred because courts and the industry misapplied stale, blunt, ethnocentric, and simplistic standards to fresh new methods of expression."[19] Walter Leaphard, manager for Public Enemy, confirms the chilling effect of cease-and-desist letters and lawsuits that have plagued the group:

> We just flat-out say, "From now on, no samples." We don't have the man power or the legal power or the money to deal with those issues. I'm still fighting and cleaning up sampling issues from 1991.[20]

The absurdity of a cultural landscape that prohibits Public Enemy from sampling has created a backlash. Copyright critics such as Vaidhyanathan argue that an artist's right to create sonic collages is guaranteed by the fair use provision of the Copyright Act. According to these critics, sampling of copyrighted recordings constitutes fair use because the resulting collages extend beyond mere copying to function as cultural critique. This argument is especially compelling because Public Enemy's 1980s recordings successfully created new meanings out of old materials. For that reason, fair use has become the rallying cry of the "Copy Left," those seeking to decrease IP restrictions on cultural expression.[21]

There is much to recommend the Copy Left's urgings to return to the spirit of the fair use provision. Fair use already exists as law; there is no need to create new legislation in order to implement it. In addition, fair use balances the needs of authors and publishers with those of other creators. A fair use exemption limits the power of copyright in order to promote cultural production, but only under

limited circumstances so that copyright can still adequately protect against piracy. For this reason, many Copy Leftists assert their
right to fair use through bold appropriations and borrowings. This
is legal but risky. The Copyright Act of 1976 and several subsequent
court decisions have interpreted fair use as an "affirmative defense,"
meaning that the burden of establishing the defense remains with
the defendants themselves.[22] In other words, the plaintiff in an
infringement suit does not have to prove that the borrowing was
"unfair"; rather the defendant must prove that it was "fair." Most
defendants in infringement cases choose to settle out of court rather
than pay attorneys' fees, and these settlements almost always require
the infringer to remove the borrowed materials from the derivative
work.[23]

Another drawback of the fair use defense is the difficulty of establishing what "fair" means. The Copyright Act lists four factors to be
weighed, one of which is the purpose of the use. Nonprofit activities,
or borrowing for the sake of criticism, comment, reporting, teaching, research, scholarship, or parody, have traditionally qualified for
the fair use exemption. But most recorded music is intended for
commercial sale. This is not to say that a for-profit work can never
count as fair use; as the Supreme Court's ruling on 2 Live Crew's
"Pretty Woman" indicates, a for-profit song could potentially qualify, provided that it display other features such as parody or criticism. Yet even the "Pretty Woman" case eventually settled out of
court, leaving no recent precedents defining the scope of fair use.
In addition, any claim that an appropriation functions as criticism
or commentary is subject to debate. Federal Court judges are not
trained as musicologists or cultural critics, and it might take a good
deal of persuasion to convince them that citations are not merely
theft.

Although insistence on the right of fair use seems as if it could lead to a new generation of Public Enemies, there is virtually no chance that the costs associated with mounting successful defenses will decrease anytime soon. Nor is it likely that Congress will refine the definition of fair use in an amendment to the Copyright Act. For the majority of musicians who appropriate, fair use is dead. But this doesn't mean that musicians should accept IP tyranny. The key to freeing American culture from excessive IP restrictions is to beat the system at its own game. Corporations like Disney and Time Warner have demonstrated with the Copyright Term Extension Act that they will spare no expense in lobbying Congress and petitioning the Supreme Court to lengthen copyright terms. Major record labels are enforcing a licensing system that charges outlandish fees for sampling well-known recordings. But there are legal and illegal ways around these barriers. Many independent, self-distributed artists sample illegally, knowing that their risk of getting sued is minimal because of their relative economic inconsequence within the music industry. Other musicians obey copyright laws by using samples that are free or cheap. For example, underground hip-hop, electronic dance music, and other obscure forms of sampladelia feature rich sampling and collage techniques that arguably surpass the best Public Enemy songs and certainly exceed anything featured on mainstream radio today.

LEGAL ALTERNATIVES: PRECLEARED SAMPLES

A major point of contention in the conflict over sampling has been the song catalog of George Clinton, the leader of the 1970s funk bands Parliament and Funkadelic. Thousands of samples have been drawn from Clinton's music, making him a ubiquitous presence in hip-hop. In 1993 Clinton released three volumes of a compilation entitled *Sample Some of Disc, Sample Some of DAT*, containing portions of already released Parliament and Funkadelic songs. These albums contain an "internal" license that is activated when the user abides by the terms stipulated in the liner notes. The terms require the user to provide Clinton's publishers with the name of the sampled track, the name of the newly created song, and the record label on which the song is to be released. This licensing agreement is unusually generous in that it requires royalty payments *only* when records are sold; no up-front royalty is required. Virtually all sample licensing agreements struck by major labels require an up-front fee, and several in recent years have asked for all moneys ahead of time because future sales are uncertain.[24] With Clinton's license, the price for a sample is either the statutory mechanical reproduction rate or a fraction thereof if the sample constitutes only a small proportion of the new song.[25]

George Clinton can license the songs for *Sample Some of Disc* because he controls their publishing copyrights and because AEM Records, the record label releasing these tracks, agrees to these terms. Yet some of the most valuable Parliament/Funkadelic music copyrights will never be made available on sample compilation volumes because they are owned not by Clinton but by his erstwhile publisher Bridgeport Music. In 1983 Clinton allegedly signed away his rights to many of his 1970s and 1980s hits (including his famous chart-topper "Atomic Dog") in order to reimburse Bridgeport for a $1 million advance. According to Bridgeport, this advance was to be paid off through royalty deductions and the transfer of song copyrights. But Bridgeport later admitted to forging Clinton's signature on the copyright transfer documents. In 1999 Clinton sued Bridgeport for control over the catalog, charging that his wife, the co-owner of the songs, never agreed to the conditions. A federal judge in Florida found against Clinton in a 2001 ruling that deprived the funk artist of songs valued at $10 million.[26] Contested ownership of song catalogs is hardly a rare occurrence in the music industry, but this particular conflict is unique because it encompasses two diametrically opposed positions toward sampling. Since 1991 Bridgeport Music has filed more than five hundred lawsuits against record labels and artists it accuses of illegally sampling Parliament and Funkadelic songs.[27] Some of these suits will either settle out of court or be dismissed, but the Sixth Circuit Court's admonition in *Bridgeport v. Dimension* to "get a license, or don't sample" has made Clinton's sample compilation volumes even more attractive as cheap, safe methods of evoking the P-Funk sound.

Perhaps in response to Clinton's *Sample Some of Disc*, some major labels now provide their own user-friendly sample compilations. For instance, Warner Music's Web site features One Stop Trax, a service offering "pre-cleared" tracks that can be licensed online. This service seems to cater primarily to filmmakers and television producers who want to license background music, but it can also help musicians seeking collage materials.[28] The selection on One Stop Trax is limited, so musicians using this service must content themselves with a thin assortment of blues, R&B/urban, punk, and country songs. For example, in May 2003 One Stop Trax offered "All Shook Down" by the Replacements. The Web page listed the label, genre, chart information, tempo (in beats per minute), type of vocal mix, and lyrics, plus a curious description of the lyrical content: "Oppression, Outlook—Cynical, Social Comment" (even anti-establishment lyrics are searchable, marketable commodities!). The only prices listed for this track were for use in film or television. The most expensive license was for use in the main title sequence (opening credits) of a commercially released motion picture, which cost $10,000 for both master and publishing rights. An end title sequence (closing credits) cost slightly less at $7,000, while any single use in the body of a film costs $5,000. Use in television or student film was considerably less, at $3,000 and $200 respectively. One Stop Trax does not list licensing fees for sampling the work in a new song;

these are determined on a case-by-case basis. Prospective sample users must fill out an online request form describing the project, the use of the sample (including whether its lyrics will be altered), whether the sample is to be reused from the master or rerecorded, and the media on which the song will be broadcast (e.g., radio, television, cable, Internet, film). The vast majority of Warner's catalog is not preapproved, so artists must call the clearance department to secure licensing for choice tracks.

But given the current sophistication of sampling technology, relying on such costly systems may not even be necessary anymore. Both amateur and professional musicians use "sample packs," collections of sounds that can be incorporated into recordings using software programs. Some sample packs feature rudimentary noises, such as a lone trumpet note or a simple four-bar drum rhythm. Others offer elaborate excerpts in a particular style like funk or techno. Sample packs like the Old School compilations provided by United Trackers BBS are derived from well-known soul and funk songs.[29] These sounds are altered enough from the original master recording that licensing is not necessary, so they are much cheaper than the source recordings (most are well under $100). Sample packs are precleared, meaning that the consumer pays licensing when purchasing the sounds and is under no obligation to pay for further use. Despite their clear financial advantages over traditional sampling, sample packs are controversial. Some sampladelia artists argue that these packs compromise musical diversity by saturating tracks with the same types of sounds. One participant in an Internet discussion of sampling packs advocated the use of "custom samples," sounds that the user creates herself:

At least by creating your very own sound for each part in your track you will be achieving 100% originality without fail. There's no right or wrong way to write music, but I believe there are always "best" and "worst" ways, "easiest" and "hardest," and in this discussion it's really between "paying attention to detail" and "using exactly what you're given." Using preset sounds for music is like using stencils to decorate a wall. The same goes for using "loops." By going a step further and ensuring that every sound is totally original by use of custom sounds, custom samples, and whole parts re-processed through effects, means that there's a whole area to music production which artists can apply themselves to.[30]

This response underscores the resilience of originality as a goal in modern composition. Most sampladelia artists do not work with sounds they have created through traditional instrumental performance. They either borrow the sounds from recordings or manufacture them with software packs that contain millions of minuscule sounds. Technically this still counts as assembly rather than "creation." But for the respondent above and for many other like-minded musicians, originality and creativity are defined by the changes an artist makes to a work, a position echoing earlier pro-originality statements by Schoenberg.

One company that provides a large variety of synthesizers and precleared sample packs is East West Sounds. Despite East West's assurances that its sounds are fully licensed, one online reviewer of the "NY Cutz" pack voiced some reservations:

Two or three of the samples in the two "Old Recordz" tracks worry me a little, license-wise. Maybe producer Vinny Zummo, who did a frankly outstanding job creating his own beats, actually reproduced (or dreamed up) these bits by hand rather than lifting them from copyrighted sources. Maybe. If you plan to use them in a released track, my advice would be to mess with them. But again, we're talking about two or three samples in a CD package that has hundreds to choose from.[31]

East West Sounds built its reputation on high-quality, precleared samples. But mere reputation was not enough to reassure Warner Music when it was preparing to release Madonna's 2003 album *American Life*. Senior management at Warner expressed some doubt concerning the clearance status of an East West keyboard sample. When East West could not provide complete documentation on the status of the sound, Warner pulled the song in question from Madonna's album.[32]

One might think that Madonna is rich enough to afford sampling any sound she wants. Yet ironically, Madonna's wealth makes her a prime target for infringement lawsuits. Session musicians who hear their work sampled in a Madonna track might want greater compensation than what their contracts originally stipulated. Her celebrity notwithstanding, Madonna is in some sense just as vulnerable to dampening effects of IP law as fledgling artists on their first recording contract. Of course, Madonna can afford considerably more in terms of licensing fees, but the potential for legal conflicts stemming from appropriation can still give pause to everyone involved in her project.

East West Sounds offers another product called "Very Processed TeeVee," a compilation of sounds derived from television broadcasts. The program was prepared by Chris Grigg, a member of Negativland, who writes:

Simultaneously organic and electronic, and very strange and engaging. Believe it or not, these all started out in life as part of one afternoon's audio output from my own personal TV set. Copyright concerns? Naah—change a thing far enough and it just isn't the same thing any more (or

even a legally protectable derivative). Five different kinds of process-
ing appear here, all of them made with the help of a couple rackmount
effects processors.[33]

Programs like Pro Tools and Acid Pro allow users to alter sounds
simply by cutting and pasting, so it's actually easy to use slightly
altered copyrighted sounds for free. For this reason, major labels
like Warner Music require their artists to keep detailed logs of their
mixing software's procedures in order to prove that the sounds were
transformed and not simply copied.[34]

ANTICOPYRIGHT GROUPS AND "SOME RIGHTS RESERVED"

Home studio sampling software is a recent development in the history of musical appropriation. But before the appearance of these
tools, collage artists were already challenging the premises of IP law
through musical appropriations. Two principal players were John
Oswald and Negativland. The Canadian audio collage artist John
Oswald refers to his compositions as "plunderphonics," or pieces
whose components are stolen (not simply borrowed) from well-
known works. Oswald explains the compositional approach in his
1993 album *Plexure* as follows:

> There are several thousand morphs, each with reference to a com-
> posite of pop hooks. These are based on correspondent similarities
> among various pieces. The reference game is potentially an infinite
> genealogy. Plexure-bits are references. Each source fragment has been
> blended with other similar fragments. The specter of appropriation
> amongst the quoted material is rampant in these aggregates. Perhaps
> this is a practical fail-safe mechanism. Any perceived infringement is
> embedded in the proof of its dire lack of originality.[35]

The source fragments Oswald seizes upon are hooks from 1980s pop songs. He points out that the majority of material in a typical pop song is itself highly derivative, and *Plexure* makes this obvious by stringing together several similar bits of material from seemingly dissimilar sources. For instance, one track merges a sung note from Madonna's "Live to Tell" with a drum break from Metallica's "Enter Sandman." Most sampladelia is based on a danceable, four-beat meter. But *Plexure* uses no regular beats or grooves, and therefore features a much higher degree of originality than its source material. *Plexure* makes its reliance on piecemeal assemblage of disparate parts apparent both in its song credits (like as "Bing Stingspreen" and "Sinéad O'Connick Jr.") and on its album cover, a photographic collage of several pop album covers (fig. 2).

The Bay Area–based group Negativland has received perhaps the most attention for its anticopyright activities. Early Negativland pieces like "Christianity Is Stupid" interspersed obscure radio and television broadcasts with studio-produced sounds to produce cutting satires. Negativland's most contentious brush with the law came in 1991, when Island Records and Warner-Chappell Music sued the group for unauthorized use of U2's "I Still Haven't Found What I'm Looking For." Negativland paired the U2 song with outtakes from Casey Kasem's *American Top 40* radio show to create a collage entitled "U2." The lyrics of "I Still Haven't Found" espouse pacifism and tolerance and have made this one of U2's most acclaimed songs. In the Negativland recasting, however, these lyrics sound pretentious and ineffectual, especially when supplemented by Negativland's own commentary. U2 front-man Bono sings, "I believe in the kingdom come, where all the colors will bleed into one," to which a member of Negativland adds, "big mess, I'll probably have to get the STP or maybe even the 409 out for that one." Another passage features a previously recorded interview with Bono in which he

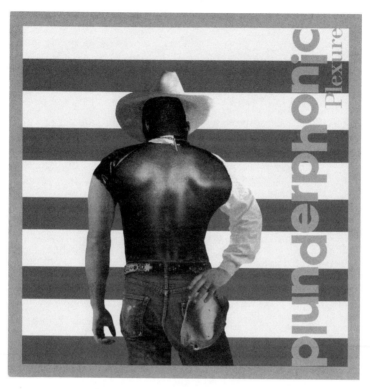

Figure 2. John Oswald's *Plexure* cover.

describes the group's interest in expanding musical horizons through the incorporation of "new sounds." When set against Negativland's low synthesizer drone, however, this interview becomes sinister, as if Bono is part of the very capitalist mechanism that his lyrics decry. Even the perennial public nice guy Kasem doesn't escape parody. Negativland juxtaposes Kasem's smooth introduction of U2 with a discarded outtake in which Kasem curses and yells at his crew for making him play an obscure "English" band (U2 is from Ireland).

Island Records and Warner-Chappell sued Negativland for trademark and copyright violations. Island claimed that the packaging for "U2," featuring a photo of the U-2 bomber airplane and the symbols "U2," violated the Lanham Act because it confused the public into believing that the Irish group U2 actually produced the recording. Island also alleged that Negativland made an unauthorized reproduction of a copyrighted U2 recording, and Warner-Chappell asserted that Negativland performed the U2 song (with kazoos) without permission.[36] Neither Negativland nor its independent distributor, SST Records, could afford the legal fees to mount a defense and were forced to settle by paying $25,000 in penalties and half the sales for the single.[37] Surprisingly, the members of U2 opposed the lawsuit and petitioned Island and Warner-Chappell to abandon their claims for damages.[38] After the settlement, SST Records attempted to recoup the $90,000 that it lost through legal fees and damages by dipping into Negativland's proceeds. Negativland retaliated by abandoning SST Records. SST struck back by launching a bizarre publicity campaign consisting of T-shirts reading "Kill Bono."

In an ironic follow-up to the Negativland debacle, U2 in 2001 granted permission and licensing to the hip-hop group Musique to sample "New Year's Day" (1983).[39] This was the first time Island Records licensed a U2 song for sampling, although unauthorized borrowings of U2 hits have appeared in underground club singles for years. One possible reason for Island's change of heart was that Musique timed its release of "New Year's Dub" to coincide with the gap between the release of the third and fourth singles from U2's 2000 album, *All That You Can't Leave Behind*. Island felt that strategic timing of the Musique song would help the sale of U2's own work. And because Musique's dance single in no way altered or added to the original message of the lyrics of "New Year's Day," Island could rest assured that U2's reputation would remain unharmed.

Since the beginning of copyright in seventeenth-century England and France, content providers have circulated the notion of individual genius in order to promote authors' moral rights and ultimately to protect their own investments in publishing.[40] This notion is difficult to dispel. Even today we tend to think of creators like Beethoven or Michelangelo as misunderstood visionaries who bore their masterpieces in a vacuum. In truth, artistic creativity is a communal act in which individuals respond to, and in many cases borrow from, each other. With their subversive works, John Oswald and Negativland have coaxed music communities into embracing and facilitating transformative appropriation. Negativland's Web site actually preaches the merits of unlicensed appropriations as *necessary* to a thriving culture.[41] In addition to descriptions of the band's many forays into sound collage and cultural critique, the site features anticopyright articles and links to groups such as ®™ark (pronounced "art mark"), a collective dedicated to funding projects that disorganize or interrupt corporate enterprises.[42] Organizations that share Negativland's enthusiasm for free musical appropriation include MACOS (Musicians Against the Copyrighting of Samples) and VirComm (Viral Communications), two consortiums whose members agree to allow their music to be sampled freely and without permission.[43] MACOS and VirComm are powered by independent musicians who control the copyrights to their own works, so they provide legal alternatives to musicians unable or unwilling to pay licensing fees. Another important Copy Left Web site is hosted by the group Illegal Art, which narrates and provides audio samples to music plagiarism cases ranging from Vanilla Ice's "Ice Ice Baby" to Biz Markie's "Alone Again."[44] Illegal Art's site also contains links to films and other banned visual works such as Todd Haynes's *Superstar: The Karen Carpenter Story* (1987), a short film using Barbie Dolls to depict the life of Karen Carpenter. Other public-advocacy Copy Left groups include the Electronic Frontier Foundation, the Center for Public Domain, Public Knowledge, and the Future of Music Coalition, all of which oppose expansions of IP law.

Of all the Copy Left organizations, the Creative Commons provides the most elegant means of enabling loosely regulated exchange of art, music, photographs, and software.[45] The nonprofit organization, founded in 2001 with the help of Copy Left advocates such as James Boyle and Lawrence Lessig, receives support from the Center for the Public Domain and the Berkman Center for Internet and Society at Harvard Law School. As its motto "Some Rights Reserved" suggests, the Creative Commons lets artists tailor copyright licenses to encourage appropriation while still allowing the originator to stipulate conditions. For instance, an author may permit free appropriation on condition of receiving credit in liner notes, or may limit use of his or her work to songs that are released on an exclusively noncommercial basis. The beauty of the Creative Commons is that it works in harmony with existing copyright laws in the United States and abroad. Licenses issued by the Creative Commons are available in three forms: as easily understandable deeds meant for artists and creators, as contracts written by lawyers, and as machine-readable deeds allowing Internet searches. Musicians who use the Creative Commons have differing aims; some want to allow free music trading among fans, while others want to make their work available for remixing and sampling. In 2003 the Creative Commons released *Copy Me, Remix Me,* a compact disc compilation of music of which free sampling is permitted. The organization has been embraced at an international level; Gilberto Gil, the Minister of Culture in Brazil, released some of his own compositions with a Creative Commons license.[46] The organization has encouraged the creation of music collectives such as Opsound (similar to MACOS) and Magnatune, a record label that distributes free copies of its artists' music. Magnatune charges money only for complete albums, shares 50 percent of all royalties with its talent, and (unlike the majority of record labels) does not own the copyrights to the music it distributes.

Although the methods of groups like MACOS and the Creative Commons are innovative, their underlying desire to incentivize transformative appropriation is far from new. Unlicensed dance remixes have long existed in both illegal and legal formats. As Simon Reynolds explains, early bootlegged remixes of star DJs were circulated on tapes that were available months before they were released commercially.[47] Producers attempted to buck this bootlegging trend by releasing authorized remix CD compilations whose proceeds guaranteed original DJs royalties. By the 1990s, it became fashionable for the producers of pop songs to commission remixes from dance club DJs. The Copy Left looks on remix culture as the most promising model for legitimate, profitable music borrowing.

SAMPLADELIA AND IP LAW

Few of today's mainstream rappers know what samples will be used on their albums before they enter the recording studio. Producers, not rappers, are usually in charge of assembling musical accompaniment to rap tracks and usually do so late in the recording process. Hip-hop celebrities routinely release *a cappella* versions of their albums in order to encourage remixing in clubs. In other words, sampling choices are often made arbitrarily in mainstream hip-hop because the composition process treats lyrics as fundamental but music as mutable, incidental, and even disposable. Sampladelia artists, by comparison, do not choose their samples arbitrarily, but rather assemble and manipulate them to create meaning and to demonstrate their connoisseurship through the savvy placement of both obscure and well-known sounds. A cornerstone of sampladelia is the notion that there is no single definitive version of a work, but this does not mean that any and all samples can be used. For instance, in performances of "scratch" hip-hop, turntable collages are improvised at live events rather than mulled over in the recording studio. A performance is judged on the merits of its mixes, and those that seem random or sloppy fail (as evidenced by distracted or jeering audiences).

Sampladelia includes music produced both by major label artists such as Beck and Moby and by amateurs and independents. Yet because sampladelia hinges on methods of borrowing and appropriation that are often illegal or prohibitively expensive, the movement is often characterized by its pro–Copy Left, anti-music-industry rhetoric. Sampladelia musicians rely on a variety of appropriation tools: turntables, analog synthesizers, digital samplers, and, increasingly, home studio software. The latter especially is democratizing sampladelia by making it affordable and accessible even to those who have no prior musical training. But the euphoria of this freedom is tempered by the sobering reality that transformative appropriation frequently carries the possibility of litigation. IP law casts a shadow on sampladelia, especially on works that clearly infringe on copyright laws. DJ Rob Fatal, a scratch artist from Sacramento, explains that in his music community, purposeful copyright infringement functions as a gesture of resistance:

> In general, hip-hop or turntablist people see not securing rights as a "fuck-you" to the industry. It's another way to rebel against the mainstream. It tells the mainstream, "you can't control our creativity and we'll steal the thing you guard so closely." Like I said, this is only some people, most hip-hop or turntablist folks just straight out don't have the money to secure the rights. The only context in which turntablist or hip-hop DJs will secure rights to songs is if they are planning major distribution, and this does not happen often.[48]

Dr. Wulf, an underground DJ and scratch promoter in San Diego, describes how copyright laws reinforce divisions between the industry and independents:

> We do "mix" available data streams of music/media/art, maybe a quote from a movie, or if a track is "hip" we'll cut that into our own unique clip. As far as securing licenses to rebroadcast, we do not. Reason being that most of our stuff is underground. Many of my DJ friends, as well as myself, do not have the time, money, expertise, or patience to deal with yet another segment of law that just seems to make the lawyers richer and make the DJs poorer. There is a fear of prosecution. That is why we promote more and more "underground" parties. We tried to go mainstream but were exploited by the labels. Sometimes just the paperwork involved was so time consuming that we would miss other lucrative underground gigs just to break even doing regular gigs. It is a business and just like a regular business, we aim to make a profit so our DJs can make money to buy more music, promotional material, stage lights, and amplifiers. The legal aspects of the music business are not evolving in line with a business of the modern world. As such, the

retainers that we used to pay to a lawyer's trust fund are better spent on equipment and music.[49]

For promoters of scratch events, underground parties are attractive alternatives to conventional concerts because they are not advertised. Attendees still pay for admission, but these events are almost never patrolled by performance rights organizations or label representatives.

Scratch competitions offer another safe space for unauthorized sampling. In these contests, DJs improvise entire songs from culled vinyl riffs and turntable punches. The most famous scratch artists today include Asian American DJs like Kuttin' Kandi, DJ QBert, and Yogafrog, who have expanded the art of turntablism through their victories at international competitions. Although scratch contests are widely publicized, they are virtually exempt from copyright licensing because monitoring independently distributed competition recordings and videos is too time consuming and expensive.[50] The critical moment in the career of an underground remix artist arrives with the decision whether to move from small-time gigs and events to mainstream distribution. Yogafrog, for instance, was forced to limit his sampling choices after achieving nationwide celebrity because his increased visibility made him a target for copyright infringement litigation.[51]

Like DJ Rob Fatal and Dr. Wulf, DJ Shadow and D-Styles handpick their samples to demonstrate their musical and cultural literacy. DJ Shadow is a Bay Area artist whose mid-1990s collages proved that hip-hop could hold its own against avant-garde music. His 1996 album *Endtroducing . . .* deftly overlays digital samples and scratches to provide what has been referred to as one of the first "ambient hop" works, ambient because the music creates landscapes of sound with repetitive electronic and acoustic figures. He mixes the usual assortment of funk and R&B with synthesizer-driven Europop (e.g., Tangerine Dream and Björk) and New Age (e.g., Windham Hill). The album cover to *Endtroducing . . .* (fig. 3) displays a record store where the center of attention is not DJ Shadow himself, but rather records and the connoisseurs who spend hours scouring used vinyl shops to find them. Ambient remix artists like DJ Shadow fashion minimalist soundscapes not unlike those of ambient composers like Brian Eno or Vangelis, but by working with samples, Shadow also invokes a sense of nostalgia for a vaguely familiar musical past.

Also hailing from the Bay Area, D-Styles is regarded as a pioneer of scratch music because of his 2003 album, *Phantazmagorea*. D-Styles performs every sound on this album by scratching; he uses no samplers or synthesizers. The cuts are drawn from a narrow band of decidedly dark material: horror films, interviews with Charles Manson and Hervé Villechaize, and documentaries on Satanism. While some tracks get bogged down with excessive displays of manual virtuosity, others create captivating new soundscapes. "Felonious Funk," for example, is an exciting quartet performed by D-Styles and three fellow scratch virtuosi, Melo-D, Babu, and DJ QBert. These turntablists control vinyl scratches well enough to produce pitched melodies (most DJs use scratching as a noise effect). The grooves in many of these songs are around seventy beats per minute—much slower than most hip-hop—permitting extremely rapid rhythmic assaults using sextuplet and thirty-second-note subdivisions.

DJ Shadow and D-Styles can both claim "underground" credibility because their music is released by independent labels with small, dedicated fan bases. Yet DJ Shadow's Mowax Recordings is owned by the prestigious A&M Records (distributed by the major Universal), which helps explain why seven samples on *Endtroducing . . .* are licensed. Presumably DJ Shadow or his label felt that these particular songs would need to be cleared to avoid lawsuits, but considering

Figure 3. DJ Shadow, cover of *Endtroducing . . .*
(courtesy of Universal Music Enterprises).

that the entire album is made up of samples, crediting merely a
handful seems perfunctory. D-Styles is distributed on an obscure
label called Beat Junkies Sound, which advertises through scratch
magazines and Internet sites, eliminating his need to license the
samples he uses.

Although sampladelia artists run the gamut from anonymous amateurs to stadium-packing superstars, a musician's distribution and
wealth determine whether he can get away with unauthorized sampling. Until recently, the trend has been for prestigious artists like
Beck and respected-but-less-distributed artists like DJ Shadow to
clear all identifiable samples, or else transform them beyond recognition. Independent artists who hope to distribute recordings beyond
their sphere of friends usually need to clear identifiable samples but
can lift more obscure ones. Amateur artists who distribute only to
local clubs and friends can get away with virtually anything. But the
2004 release of the *Grey Album* remix demonstrates the potential

of collage music to bridge the mainstream/underground chasm because the work borrowed from one of the music industry's sacred cows, the Beatles.

Unlike the works of DJ Rob Fatal, D-Styles, or even DJ Shadow, the *Grey Album* has received plenty of publicity. Its unexpected celebrity has brought copyright issues to the public's attention in a way that no other independent musician has previously. To create the *Grey Album*, Los Angeles resident DJ Danger Mouse (Brian Burton) mixed an *a cappella* version of Jay-Z's 2003 *Black Album* with instrumental loops from the Beatles' 1968 *White Album*. The *Grey Album* displays a level of sophistication that far exceeds the odd-couple pairings of most mash-ups.[52] The opening track "Public Service Announcement" begins with a looping of an organ and acoustic guitar portion of George Harrison's ballad "It's Been a Long Time." Danger Mouse adds beats constructed of percussion hits culled exclusively from the *White Album*. Jay-Z's rap enters, and amazingly, it fits. The resulting track is engaging both intellectually and emotionally; Harrison's instrumental parts reveal a poignant vulnerability that lurks beneath Jay-Z's puffed-up bragging. And unlike novelty mash-ups such as the Destiny's Child/Nirvana pairing "Smells Like Booty," the *Grey Album* involves more than a simple synchronization of the Beatles samples with Jay-Z's tracks. "Dirt off Your Shoulder," for instance, opens with an acoustic guitar groove plus John Lennon's wordless vocals from "Julia." This groove suddenly disintegrates when Burton shatters the "Julia" loop into myriad split-second samples, which he then assembles into new rhythms and melodies. The pitches of some of these samples are shifted up or down, allowing Burton to depart from the original "Julia" melody even while retaining its timbres and contours. Burton treats the Beatles songs as palettes from which he draws out individual colors. Refashioning these sounds and reorganizing them into new sonic phrases and sentences, he creates acoustic mosaics that in most instances are still traceable to the Beatles source, yet are unmistakably distinct from it.

The *Grey Album* stands out not only for its own musical merits, but also because it has introduced issues of musical creativity and intellectual property to mainstream music consumers. Burton released three thousand promotional copies of the work in December 2003, and in February 2004 he received a cease-and-desist letter from EMI, the copyright owner of the master tapes to the Beatles' *White Album*. EMI also threatened legal action to any individuals who sold or transmitted copies of the *Grey Album* over eBay or through file-sharing networks. Public outcry against EMI came to a head on March 5, 2004, when Copy Left advocates Downhill Battle and Kembrew McLeod hosted "Grey Tuesday." This event protested EMI's threats by inviting participants to download free copies of the *Grey Album*. Affiliated Web sites featured analyses of the IP issues at stake, as well as a sample letter retort in case EMI threatened the downloader with litigation. "Grey Tuesday" was widely reported by media outlets such as CNN, MTV, and *Rolling Stone*, and university radio stations expressed their support by playing the *Grey Album*, the Beatles' *White Album*, and Jay-Z's original mix of the *Black Album*. In March 2004, Burton complied with EMI's demands and stopped selling and distributing copies of the work, but this gesture was irrelevant considering that the Illegal Art Web site was still offering free downloads of the album.[53]

The Electronic Frontier Foundation (EFF) posted a detailed analysis of the legal issues posed by the *Grey Album* and the "Grey Tuesday" protest.[54] Because the *White Album* was recorded in 1968 (before music recordings were grandfathered into U.S. federal copyright), EMI would probably have succeeded only in claiming *state* copyright protection for the tapes. The compositions on the *White Album* are covered under federal copyright, and most are owned by

Sony/ATV. The EFF noted that in the lawsuit *Newton v. Diamond*, the Ninth Circuit Court found that the Beastie Boys' sampling of James Newton's recording did not constitute a copyright infringement because the snippet of flute music was too insignificant to be a substantial borrowing. The Court termed this a "fragmented literal similarity," meaning that the borrowed sounds were reordered in such a way as to depart significantly from the original. Since most of the samples on the *Grey Album* are also dramatically restructured from their sources on the *White Album*, DJ Danger Mouse could have claimed this defense had he been brought to trial. EFF's analysis concerned itself mostly with the "Grey Tuesday" protesters, however, and whether they could claim their uploading or downloading of the *Grey Album* as a fair use. Although the EFF page supported a fair use defense, it cautioned that there was little case-law precedent for distributing, as a social protest, a work that potentially violated copyright.

The production and distribution of the *Grey Album* did not lead to any outright lawsuits, just cease-and-desist letters. The aesthetic integrity of DJ Danger Mouse's artwork alerted the general public to inconsistencies in the copyright regime. In future years, the *Grey Album* will probably be seen as a highly visible first step in a public backlash against IP extremism. Previous mash-ups disparaged their source materials, so critics could always dismiss them as musical jokes lacking real substance or creativity. But the *Grey Album* paid homage to both the Beatles and Jay-Z, and fans of both expressed admiration for the project. The *Grey Album* also had marketing potential in a way that other underground remixing does not; the controversial mixing of "black" rap and "white" prestige rock nearly sold itself. Remarkably, Jay-Z and his record label, Rock-a-fella Records, have tacitly supported DJ Danger Mouse by not serving cease-and-desist letters of their own. Danger Mouse created the *Grey Album* in the first place because Jay-Z released an *a cappella* version of his *Black Album* in order to encourage remixing.

COMPULSORY LICENSING FOR SAMPLING

Some legal theorists have proposed amending the Copyright Act with a compulsory license for sampling in an attempt to facilitate the licensing process. Chris Johnstone has suggested a "sampling tax": producers who sample would pay the Copyright Office a statutory fee based on the number of recordings they sell.[55] The Copyright Office would then distribute royalties from tax proceeds proportionally to copyright holders of sampled materials based on how often their works were reused in a year. This plan eliminates any confusion between piracy and sampling. In defining sampling clearly as a transformative use, this compulsory licensing plan would render obsolete the types of lawsuits that even now are still common, wherein producers argue over whether a sampling occurred and whether it was transformative or plagiaristic. This tax would also remove the need for copyright clearance companies that charge hefty fees to undertake negotiations.

Ironically, the strength of this plan is the very reason why it will never be implemented: it proposes a statutory rate that would reduce the standard fees for sample licensing considerably. For instance, Johnstone discusses a hypothetical example of a sample-filled song that has sold 100 million copies. The producer of this song is required to pay $27,500 to license all samples, a fraction of what high-profile samples currently cost. But of that amount, only $2,750 is paid to the copyright holder of a particular sampled song, because individual payments would be calculated according to the rate at which a specific track is borrowed. Naturally, the copyright holders for desirable catalogs such as those of James Brown or Parliament/Funkadelic

would balk at this meager figure because under the current system, a
label is virtually free to name any price as an up-front charge. Despite
the elegance of Johnstone's proposal, this plan probably cannot be
integrated into the Copyright Act because it would encounter too
much resistance from the recording industry.

Christopher D. Abramson has suggested an alternative plan, a
conventional statutory license that addresses performers' rights as
well as those of copyright holders.[56] Currently the American Fed-
eration of Musicians (AFM) operates under a contract with record
companies whereby copyright holders are required to pay a lump-
sum fee to the AFM whenever one of their songs is sampled. The
AFM then distributes this fee among its members. This agreement
usually does not provide reimbursement for nonfeatured musicians
who accompany a headlining artist. Abramson proposes a statutory
property right for all musicians that would ensure compensation for
both featured and nonfeatured musicians. This plan seems even less
promising than the Johnstone proposal because it would raise the
price of sampling as a way of encouraging producers to use live musicians. Given the ease and affordability of sampling, the recording
industry is unlikely to adopt an expensive performers' rights policy.

With increasing restrictions on musical appropriation and contract terms prohibiting performers from controlling their own material, the prognosis for major label musicians is grim. Few fledgling
artists can hope to approach anything like the mind-boggling commercial success of David Bowie or Michael Jackson. Yet these daunting prospects for financial gain might yield unexpected benefits for
the future of music. The figure of the rock superstar that became
commonplace during the 1970s and 1980s is anomalous. Until quite
recently, musicians never earned large sums of money; the era of the
highly paid musician began arguably in the nineteenth century with
virtuosi like Franz Liszt, and it seems to be drawing to a close in

the early twenty-first century. In past decades, signing with a major label was tantamount to sure financial success, but the majority of artists who work under the majors today end up losing money (even if they don't appropriate any music).[57] Artists who decide to work with smaller labels or who distribute their own work may give up wide circulation, but they gain control over the copyrights to their own work. Artists who appropriate from works made available through Creative Commons licensing can bypass expensive permissions and ultimately exercise greater control over the final product than can their major-label colleagues.

Some successful, prestigious artists have embraced innovative modes of transformative appropriation that may augur a sea change for the music industry at large. On April 16, 2004, David Bowie sponsored a mash-up competition in which participants were challenged to remix a song from his new album *Reality* with any other Bowie song.[58] The rules required all contestants to work with recordings they themselves had purchased in order to prevent piracy. Second- and third-place prizes included remixing software and computers; the grand prize was a 2004 Audi TT Coupe. By supporting transformative appropriation, Bowie again proved his aptitude for engaging with the most cutting-edge trends in music. And by uniting with a luxury automobile company like Audi, Bowie showed that transformative appropriation can thrive even with corporate support. Admittedly, this example would bear more relevance to the topic at hand if Bowie had allowed participants to hold copyrights over their remixes; as it was, Bowie retained full ownership and control over all materials produced through the competition.

Given the variable and often contradictory relationship between musical appropriation and IP law, the task of categorizing our current musical culture in unilaterally positive or negative terms is impossible. But we should ask ourselves, what kind of musical culture do we want in the future? Before answering, consider the type of musical culture we will have if we sit back and let content providers continue to run the show. Many of the laws and lawsuits described in this book share one disturbing feature: the desire to preserve the legacies of deceased entertainers. The right of publicity in California originally developed to protect the identities of dead celebrities from commercial adaptation, and was only later applied to the living. The Copyright Term Extension Act of 1998 (named after Sonny Bono, who before his untimely death was said to have favored *perpetual* copyrights) extended copyright terms seventy years beyond the death of authors, ensuring that many works created today will lapse into the public domain no sooner than the twenty-second century, at which point most of us will be dead anyway. John Cage possessed a keen sense of humor, and were he alive today, he might well have supported Mike Batt's invocation of his silent piece. Yet because Cage is now unreachable in the silence of the grave, Peters Edition can protect his name as fiercely as if it were its own. If the music and film industries had their way, our artistic heritage would be a mausoleum in which sounds and images are frozen in time, impervious to appropriation.

Today's permissions culture, in which we pay for every viewing, listening, and borrowing, would perhaps have been better suited to consumer habits of the 1950s and 1960s, when record listening first replaced home music performance. But the ease of home remixing is returning us to a more participatory model of music making. In the world of sampladelia, listening and composition go hand in hand: artists engage with music through both passive contemplation and active appropriation. At the moment, legal and affordable ways to make transformative musical appropriations still exist, and some American courts have demonstrated if not unconditional acceptance, then at least a willingness to tolerate forms of borrowing that depart significantly from originals. But if the *Bridgeport v. Dimension* decision and the *Grey Album* controversy are indicative of the future, unauthorized remixing will become an outlawed activity, and content providers will continue to lobby for increasing (and possibly perpetual) copyright terms. And if David Bowie's mash-up competition is the only model of corporate-sanctioned transformative appropriation, remixing will remain a permissions-based activity wherein the copyright holder approaches transformers, not vice versa. Copy Left artists like DJ Danger Mouse and Negativland have persisted under the shadow of IP law to produce engaging art. Their image is a heroic one, but it should not distract us from the potential of IP law to silence and deaden our future musical culture.

NOTES

INTRODUCTION

1. But as chapter 2 explains, certain iconic *sounds* have qualified for trademark protection—e.g., the MGM lion's roar or the NBC station identification chime.

2. Boyle, *Shamans, Software, and Spleens*; Coombe, *The Cultural Life of Intellectual Properties*; Lessig, *Free Culture*; McLeod, *Freedom of Expression®*; Vaidhyanathan, *Copyrights and Copywrongs*.

3. McLeod, *Owning Culture*, ix–xv.

4. McLeod, *Freedom of Expression®*.

5. "Silent Music Dispute Resolved," *BBC News*; "Composer Pays for Piece of Silence," CNN; Greenman, "The Talk of the Town," 48.

6. "John Cage Silence," *Peters Edition*.

7. *Grand Upright Music, Ltd. v. Warner Brothers Records*, 780 F. Supp. 182 (S.D.N.Y. 1991).

8. McLeod, *Owning Culture*; Vaidhyanathan, *Copyrights and Copywrongs*.

9. Lessig, *Free Culture*.

10. Mnookin and Kornhauser, *Bargaining in the Shadow of the Law*.

CHAPTER ONE. MUSIC AS INTELLECTUAL PROPERTY

1. "The Stuntman," Respect Copyrights Web site.

2. Makeen, *Copyright in a Global Information Society*, 5.

3. Kaplan, *An Unhurried View of Copyright*, 3.

4. As Lawrence Lessig points out, it took until 1774 for the Statute of Anne to be upheld in English courts. Lessig, *Free Culture*, 85–94.

5. Makeen, *Copyright in a Global Information Society*, 7–15.

6. Locke, "On Property," Chap. 5, sec. 27.

7. U.S. Constitution, art. 1, sec. 8.

8. *Copyright Act of May 21, 1790*, 1st Cong., 2d Sess., *U.S. Statutes at Large* 1:124.

9. Patry, "The First Copyright Act." Patry points out that the first copyright for a musical composition was granted on January 6, 1794, for "The Kentucky Volunteer: A New Song," attributed to Raynor Taylor.

10. *Copyright Act of February 3, 1831*, 21st Cong., 2d Sess., *U.S. Statutes at Large* 4:436.

11. *Dramatic Compositions Copyright Act of August 18, 1856*, 34th Cong., 1st Sess., *U.S. Statutes at Large* 11:138.

12. *Act of January 6, 1897*, 44th Cong., 2d Sess., *U.S. Statutes at Large*, 29:481.

13. Makeen, *Copyright in a Global Information Society*, 22.

14. Sanjek, *Pennies from Heaven*, 32ff.

15. A "work for hire" is a category of creative work defined by the copyright act that includes multi-author works like motion pictures, literary anthologies, and atlases. See *Copyright Act, U.S. Code* 17 (1976), sec. 101.

16. Merges, Menell, and Lemley, *Intellectual Property in the New Technology Age*, 396.

17. *Sound Recording Act of 1971*, Public Law 92-170, 92d Cong., 1st sess. (October 15, 1971), *U.S. Statutes at Large* 85: 391. The 1976 Copyright Act altered this slightly by stating that all recordings created on or after January 1, 1978, receive federal protection, regardless of whether they are published or unpublished. Recordings made prior to February 15, 1972, or unpublished prior to January 1, 1978, receive protection under state common law until February 15, 2047, after which time they will lapse into the public domain. Krasilovsky and Shemel, *This Business of Music*, 96–97.

18. Lessig, *Free Culture*, 170–71.

19. Lessig, *Free Culture*, 53–61; Vaidhyanathan, *Copyrights and Copywrongs*, 1–3.

20. Goldstein, *International Copyright*, 23.

21. During the nineteenth century, several European countries formulated international copyright treaties that culminated with the Berne Con-

vention of 1883. The membership for this treaty later expanded to include former European colonies in Africa and South America. For the framers of the Berne Convention, copyright was a natural right that belonged to all authors from the time of creation onward. Copyright was therefore felt not to be contingent on formalities such as depositing works with the government, or listing the copyright symbol. The United States insisted throughout most of its history that formality requirements helped avoid unnecessary litigation, but it softened its stance when it chose to enter the Berne Convention in 1988. The Berne Convention Implementation Act synchronizes the United States with other Berne members by loosening the requirements for registration, notice, publication, and deposit. See Merges, Menell, and Lemley, *Intellectual Property in the New Technology Age*, 443; Krasilovsky and Shemel, *This Business of Music*, 227; *Berne Convention Implementation Act of 1988*, Public Law 100-568, 100th Cong., 2d sess. (October 31, 1988).

The World Intellectual Property Organization (WIPO) in 1996 issued a treaty that establishes minimum copyright protection standards for digital media such as computer software. This treaty prohibits the deletion of digital safeguards against infringement such as encryption and watermarking devices. The treaty is also the first international agreement to distinguish between ideas, which it views as free and unprotectable, and expressions, which can be copyrighted. This distinction between ideas and expressions is the cornerstone of American copyright law, but before the WIPO Treaty, most European nations resisted the concept. The WIPO also issued the Performances and Phonograms Treaty, which stipulates that both composers and performers receive "rights of attribution and integrity" in their live aural performances or performances fixed in phonograms. This acknowledgment stems directly from the doctrine of moral rights, which grants to authors not only economic power over their work but also the right to determine its usage. This inclusion was notable because it was the first time that moral rights pertaining to performers (as opposed to authors) were included in an international agreement. The WIPO Performances and Phonograms Treaty poses a potentially dangerous extension of copyright protection because it would allow performers to prohibit the creation of parodies of their work. These concerns notwithstanding, the United States imposed its own Digital Millennium Copyright Act (DMCA) of 1998 to comply with the WIPO treaty. The goal of the DMCA is to ensure legal Internet distribution of copyrighted works by securing digital networks. It does this by forbidding attempts to circumvent or destroy technologies that would disallow illegal copying or distribution of protected content. The DMCA also indemnifies Internet service providers (ISPs) whose customers transmit infringed materials, but on the condition that the ISPs remove the materials from Web sites upon direction from the Copyright Office. See Goldstein, *International Copyright: Principles, Law, and Practice*, 43; Vaidhyanathan, *Copyrights and Copywrongs*, 162; Littman, *Digital Copyright*, 122–50.

22. *Copyright Act, U.S. Code* 17 (1976), sec. 107.

23. Foucault, "What Is an Author?" 123.

24. Schoenberg, "Folklorist Symphonies," 165.

25. George, *Hip-hop America*, 96.

26. McLeod, *Owning Culture*, 39–70; Floyd, *The Power of Black Music*, 95.

27. Gates, *The Signifying Monkey*.

28. Horncastle, "Plagiarism," 147.

29. Horncastle, "Plagiarism," 141.

30. Von Sternberg, "On Plagiarism," 391.

31. Scott, "Indebtedness in Music," 502.

32. Geller, *Hiroshige vs. Van Gogh*.

CHAPTER TWO. ARRANGEMENTS AND MUSICAL ALLUSION

1. Soocher, *They Fought the Law*, 1–20.

2. Doss, *Elvis Culture*, 216.

3. Music historians use the term "Romantic" to describe European concert music from around 1800 to 1900 (roughly simultaneous with the British literary Romantic period) that displayed extreme emotional expression.

4. Vaudeville was a form of light entertainment popular in Europe and the Americas in the early twentieth century, featuring music, comedy, acrobatics, and stage antics. Tin Pan Alley refers to the songwriting and music publishing business centered in New York from the 1890s to the 1950s. Many songs created in Tin Pan Alley were taken on tour in Vaudeville productions.

5. Thornton, *Club Cultures*, 34–50; Lanza, *Elevator Music*, 46.

6. As Brian Wards states, "few fans wanted the sheet music to 'Maybel-

line'—they wanted Chuck Berry's Chess record, the specific performance."
Ward, *Just My Soul Responding*, 43.

7. Gracyk, *Rhythm and Noise*, ix. Christopher Small would disagree: "On the contrary, *performance is the primary process of musicking*, from which all other processes follow" (his italics). Small is correct at an ontological level: a recording exists only after someone has taken the trouble of performing the music. Since this book deals with IP laws, I am concerned primarily with objects like recordings that can be owned and sold. Small, *Musicking*, 113.

8. Merges, Menell, and Lemley, *Intellectual Property in the New Technology Age*, 336.

9. Small, *Musicking*, 112–13.

10. *White-Smith Music Publishing Co. v. Apollo Co.*, 209 U.S. 1 (1908).

11. Sanjek and Sanjek, *American Popular Music Business in the Twentieth Century*, 12.

12. Krasilovsky and Shemel, *This Business of Music*, 111.

13. *Copyright Act, U.S. Code* 17 (1976), sec. 115(2).

14. *Copyright Act, U.S. Code* 17 (1976), sec. 106(2).

15. *Copyright Act, U.S. Code* 17 (1976), sec. 101.

16. Krasilovsky and Shemel, *This Business of Music*, 148.

17. Gracyk, *Rhythm and Noise*, 96.

18. Gaines, *Contested Culture*, 121.

19. *Copyright Act of 1831*, 21st Cong., 2d sess. (February 3, 1831), 4 Stat. 436.

20. *The New Grove Dictionary of Music and Musicians*, 2d ed., s.v. "Arrangement" (by Malcolm Boyd), http://www.grovemusic.com (accessed November 12, 2003).

21. King, "The Anatomy of a Jazz Recording," 294.

22. Lowe, "Claiming Amadeus," 102–19.

23. Adorno, "On the Fetish Character in Music and the Regression of Listening," 298–99.

24. Gendron, *Between Montmartre and the Mudd Club*, 172–74.

25. Lanza, *Elevator Music*, 27.

26. The rhythm of this motto can be described as "short-short-short-long." The rhythm's similarity to the Morse code for the letter 'V' made the symphony popular in Great Britain during World War II.

27. Thom Bell was the producer for Philadelphia International Records, an independent record label responsible for several "soft soul" recordings of the early and mid-1970s. Bell's arrangements influenced later disco tracks.

28. A vibraslap is a percussion instrument that imitates the sound of a rattlesnake.

29. Emerson, review of *Saturday Night Fever: The Original Movie Soundtrack*.

30. Lowe, "Claiming Amadeus," 102ff.

31. Prendergast, *The Ambient Century*, 71.

32. See Baraka, *Black Music*, 207; Maultsby, "Beginnings of a Black Music Industry," xi; Ward, *Just My Soul Responding*, 45–46.

33. Doss, *Elvis Culture*, 174; Ward, *Just My Soul Responding*, 47–48.

34. George, *The Death of Rhythm and Blues*, 63.

35. Middleton, "All Shook Up?" 151–61.

36. *Oxford English Dictionary Online*, 2d ed., s.v. "parody" and "satire."

37. See *Shapiro, Bernstein & Co. v. P.F. Collier & Son Co.*, 26 USPQ 40 (S.D.N.Y. 1934), in which the court ruled that parodic appropriation of song choruses for use in a magazine article counted as fair use.

38. *Copyright Act, U.S. Code* 17 (1976), sec. 107.

39. *Campbell v. Acuff-Rose*, 510 U.S. 569 (1994).

40. Patry, *The Fair Use Privilege in Copyright Law*, 195.

41. *Acuff-Rose Music Inc. v. Campbell*, 754 F. Supp. 1150 (MD Ten. 1991). The defendants' move for summary judgment was based on their claim that 2 Live Crew's borrowing of "Oh, Pretty Woman" was legal. A summary judgment bypasses the trial altogether, so it is a way for a judge to rule on the reasonability of the allegations before the case can proceed.

42. *Acuff-Rose Music Inc. v. Campbell*, 972 F.2d 1429 (6th Cir. 1992).

43. *Campbell v. Acuff-Rose*, 510 U.S. 569 (1994).

44. Merges, Menell, and Lemley, *Intellectual Property in the New Technology Age*, 481.

45. Sutcliffe, "Oasis."

46. For a discussion of space-age bachelor pad music and its revival in the 1990s, see Taylor, *Strange Sounds*, 72–116.

47. Jonathan Z. King suggests that some courts may potentially object to arrangements that depart from the fundamental character of their original

source material, but he also points out that this distinction has not been tested in recent rulings. King, "The Anatomy of a Jazz Recording," 291–92.

48. *Sinatra v. Goodyear Tire and Rubber Co.*, 435 F.2d 711 (1970).

49. Gaines, *Contested Culture*, 114–15.

50. *Midler v. Ford Motor Co.*, U.S. Dist. Lexis 14367 (C.D. Ca. 1987); *Midler v. Ford Motor Co.*, 849 F.2d 460 (9th Cir. 1988).

51. Gaines, *Contested Culture*, 141.

52. *Waits v. Frito-Lay*, 978 F.2d 1093 (9th Cir. 1991).

53. McLeod, *Owning Culture*, 215.

54. Doss, *Elvis Culture*, 229.

55. *Tin Pan Apple, Inc. v. Miller Brewing Co.*, 737 F. Supp. 826 (S.D.N.Y. 1990); *Tin Pan Apple, Inc. v. Miller Brewing Co.*, U.S. Dist. LEXIS 2178 (S.D.N.Y. 1994).

56. "Eminem Sues Apple, MTV Over iTunes Ad," *USA Today*.

57. Werde, "Could I Get That in Elvis, Please?" *New York Times*, sec. 2.

58. Lhamon, *Raising Cain*.

CHAPTER THREE. DUPLICATION

1. Benjamin, "The Work of Art in the Age of Mechanical Reproduction," 221.

2. Béthune, *Le rap*, 9; Goodwin, "Sample and Hold," 258–73.

3. Baudrillard, *Simulacra and Simulation*.

4. Schaeffer, *De la musique concrète à la musique même*, 37ff; Pellman, *An Introduction to the Creation of Electroacoustic Music*, 52, 329–31; Watkins, *Soundings*, 584.

5. Taylor, *Strange Sounds*, 46; Schaeffer, *À la recherche d'une musique concrète*.

6. Taylor, *Strange Sounds*, 60–61; Prendergast, *The Ambient Century*, 44–49, 117.

7. Miller, "Dickie Goodman"; Gordon and Sanders, *When Parodies Use Musical Allusion to Copyrighted Works*.

8. Barnett, "The Monster and the Mash-up"; Cruger, "The Mash-up Revolution."

9. Coombe, *The Cultural Life of Intellectual Properties*, 88–129.

10. Once Michael Jackson and Sony/ATV bought the publishing rights to the Lennon/McCartney catalog, this "Revolution" was used in a Nike advertising campaign in 1986, much to the consternation of McCartney and Ono.

11. Lawrence, *Love Saves the Day*, 214–16.

12. Demers, "Sampling the 1970s in Hip-hop," 41–56.

13. Gates, *The Signifying Monkey*, 44ff.

14. See Walser, "Out of Notes," 343–65; Murphy, "Jazz Improvisation," 32–47; Tomlinson, "Cultural Dialogics and Jazz," 64–78.

15. George, *Buppies, B-Boys, Baps and Bohos*, 4.

16. Dr. Dre, "Let Me Ride," *The Chronic*, Death Row 63000, 1992.

17. Peters, *Lyrics of the Afro-American Spiritual*.

18. Brennan, "Off the Gangsta Tip," 681.

19. Leeds, "Dispute over Sampling," C1.

20. Lauryn Hill, "Doo Wop (That Thing)," *The Miseducation of Lauryn Hill*, Sony 69035, 1998.

21. Baraka and Amina Baraka, "The Phenomenon of Soul in African-American Music," 269–75.

22. Dark, "Push in the Bush," 75.

23. Dark, "Push in the Bush," 75.

24. Tom Tom Club, "Genius of Love," *Tom Tom Club*, Warner 3628, 1981.

25. Elflein, "From Krauts with Attitudes to Turks with Attitudes," 255–65.

26. Swedenberg, "Homies in the 'Hood," 55.

27. Smith, " 'I Don't Like to Dream about Getting Paid,' " 69–97.

28. George, *Hip-hop America*, 94.

29. Marcus, *Don't Stop That Funky Beat*, 767–90.

30. Vaidhyanathan, *Copyrights and Copywrongs*, 132–33.

31. Snowden, "Sampling," 61; McLeod, *Owning Culture*, 87; Hochman, "Judge Raps Practice of 'Sampling,' " F1.

32. *Grand Upright Music, Ltd. v. Warner Brothers Records*, 780 F. Supp. 182 (S.D.N.Y. 1991).

33. *Grand Upright v. Warner*, 8. The pertinent criminal codes are found in *U.S. Code 17*, sec. 506(a), and *U.S. Code 18*, sec. 2319.

34. Harrington, "The Groove Robbers' Judgment," D1; Lichtman, "Suit vs. Biz Markie Settled," 80.

35. George, *Hip-hop America*, 95.

36. *Boyd Jarvis v. A&M Records*, 827 F. Supp. 282 (D.C. New Jersey 1992).

37. Douglass and Mende, "Music Sampling," 23–28.

38. *Tuff 'N' Rumble Management Inc. v. Profile Records Inc.*, 42 U.S.P.Q. 2d (S.D.N.Y. 1997).

39. *Williams v. Broadus*, U.S. Dist. LEXIS 12894 (S.D.N.Y. 2001).

40. *Newton v. Diamond*, 204 F. Supp. 2d 1244 (D.C. Calif. 2002).

41. A multiphonic is produced by "overblowing" into the flute embouchure, creating a combination of two or even three notes simultaneously. Flutists can sing while blowing into the flute, but this occurs infrequently in Western classical music and only occasionally in jazz.

42. Boucher, "A Musician Writes It, a Rapper Borrows It," F1; Newton, "An Open Letter from Musician James Newton."

43. *Newton v. Diamond*, 349 F.3d 591 (9th Cir. 2003).

44. *Bridgeport v. Dimension*, 230 F. Supp. 2d 830 (MD Ten. 2002).

45. *Bridgeport v. Dimension*, 383 F.3d 390 (6th Cir. 2004).

46. McLeod, *Owning Culture*, 99; Vaidhyanathan, *Copyrights and Copywrongs*, 144–45.

47. Ice Cube, "Jackin' for Beats," *Kill At Will*, Priority Records 7230, 1990.

48. Vaidhyanathan, *Copyrights and Copywrongs*, 143.

49. For discussions of the various forms of electronic music, see Bogdanov and others, *All Music Guide to Electronica*; Reynolds, *Generation Ecstasy*; Shapiro, *Modulations*.

50. Reynolds, *Generation Ecstasy*, 41.

51. Agawu, *Playing with Signs*, 49.

52. Considerations of Simon's *Graceland* include Erlmann, *African Stars*; Hamm, *Putting Popular Music in Its Place*, 336–43; Kivnick, *Where Is the Way?*; Meintjes, "Paul Simon's *Graceland*," 37–74.

53. Feld, "Notes on 'World Beat,'" 239; Hamm, *Putting Popular Music in Its Place*; Lipsitz, *Dangerous Crossroads*.

54. Frith, "Music and Morality," 8.

55. Mills, "Indigenous Music and the Law," 57–86; Zemp, "The/An Ethnomusicologist and the Record Business," 36–56.

56. Nancy Guy, "Trafficking in Taiwan Aboriginal Voices," 195–209; Taylor, *Strange Sounds*, 117–35.

57. Chadha, "Mix This."

58. The song is called "Thoda Resham Lagta Hai."

59. Kaufman, "Judge Rules Truth Hurts' Album Must Be Pulled or Stickered."

60. Miller, "Loops of Perception."

61. Wall, *EST Magazine* interview.

62. Miller, "Loops of Perception"; Wall, *EST Magazine* interview.

63. Harvey, *The Condition of Postmodernity*; Jameson, *Postmodernism*; Kramer, *Classical Music and Postmodern Knowledge*.

64. Finell, *How a Musicologist Views Digital Sampling Issues*.

CHAPTER FOUR. THE SHADOW OF THE LAW

1. Sebald, *Austerlitz*, 286.

2. Bridges, "Rip, Mix and Burn."

3. Coombe, *The Cultural Life of Intellectual Properties*.

4. Interview with Nanette Simon, *Willful Infringement: A Report from the Front Lines of the Real Culture Wars*, DVD, directed by Greg Hittelman (Fiat Lucre: 2003).

5. In addition to the titles already mentioned, see Bettig, *Copyrighting Culture*; David Bollier, *Brand Name Bullies*; Boyle, *Shamans, Software, and Spleens*.

6. Brabec and Brabec, *Music, Money, and Success*, 393–99.

7. "Statutory Mechanical Royalty Rates," *The Harry Fox Agency, Inc.*

8. Krasilovsky and Shemel, *This Business of Music*, 177–79.

9. "Contractual Issues," *The Recording Artists' Coalition*.

10. McLeod, *Owning Culture*, 27.

11. Morgan, "Copywrong."

12. There are numerous excoriations of the copyright of "Happy Birthday," including those in Mikkelson and Mikkelson, "Happy Birthday, We'll Sue."

13. David Hunt (Diamond Time Ltd.), telephone conversation with author, September 11, 2002.

14. McLeod, *Owning Culture*, 91.

15. Taraska, "Sampling Remains."

16. Derrick Finch (jazz pianist in Los Angeles), personal communication, April 7, 2003.

17. Boucher, "A Musician Writes It, a Rapper Borrows It," F1.

18. McLeod, "How Copyright Law Changed Hip Hop."

19. Vaidhyanathan, *Copyrights and Copywrongs*, 144.

20. Interview with Walter Leaphard, *Willful Infringement*.

21. Boynton, "The Tyranny of Copyright?" 40.

22. Patry, *The Fair Use Privilege in Copyright Law*, 585.

23. Chuck D explains: "Public Enemy was affected because it is too expensive to defend against a claim. So we had to change our whole style." McLeod, "How Copyright Law Changed Hip Hop."

24. Mark Goldstein (vice president, Warner Music), in discussion with the author, September 2003.

25. George Clinton, *Sample Some of Disc—Sample Some of DAT*, AEM Record Group 25741-2, 1993.

26. Leeds, "Dispute over Sampling Fees Has George Clinton in a Legal Funk," C1.

27. Hochman and Philips, "Pop Eye," 69.

28. One Stop Trax, http://www.onestoptrax.com (accessed May 9, 2003).

29. United Trackers BBS, http://www.united-trackers.org (accessed May 29, 2003).

30. Anonymous email to Sampling group, October 15, 2002, http://alt.music.makers.sampling.

31. Aikin, Review of "NY Cutz."

32. Mark Goldstein, interview.

33. Grigg, "Very Processed TeeVee."

34. Mark Goldstein, interview.

35. Oswald, "Plunderstanding Ecophonomics," 9–17.

36. Negativland, *Fair Use*, 4–7.

37. Sloop and Herman, "Negativland," 295–96. Island later allegedly offered to return rights for "U2" back to Negativland if Kasem would sign

an agreement pledging he wouldn't sue the label. Kempfert, "Negativland Climb the Highest Mountain."

38. Negativland, *Fair Use*, 32.

39. "U2 sample clearance," *Music Week*.

40. Battersby, *Gender and Genius*.

41. Negativland, http://www.negativland.com (accessed May 28, 2003).

42. In one such prank, ®™ark paid participants to buy Barbie and G.I. Joe dolls, switch their voice chips, and return them to stores, where they were resold with Barbie talking in army jargon and G.I. Joe proclaiming a love of shopping. This project was called the "Barbie Liberation Organization," or "B.L.O." for short. "B.L.O.," ®™ark, http://www.rtmark.com/blo.html (accessed May 22, 2004).

43. MACOS, http://www.icomm.ca/macos (accessed April 19, 2003); VirComm, http://detritus.net/vircomm/ (accessed May 27, 2003).

44. Illegal Art, http://www.illegal-art.org (accessed May 22, 2004).

45. Creative Commons, http://creativecommons.org/projects/sampling (accessed May 22, 2004).

46. Boynton, "The Tyranny of Copyright?" 44.

47. Reynolds, *Generation Ecstasy*, 276–77.

48. DJ Rob Fatal, in discussion with the author, April 18, 2003.

49. Dr. Wulf, in discussion with the author, April 9, 2003.

50. DJ Rob Fatal, in discussion with the author, April 18, 2003.

51. Yogafrog, in conversation with interviewer Juliana Snapper, October 2002.

52. Moss, "*Grey Album* Producer Danger Mouse Explains How He Did It."

53. Sony/ATV, the owner of the Lennon/McCartney composition copyrights, sent a Digital Millennium Copyright Act take-down notice to Illegal Art's Internet service provider. "The *Grey Album* Story So Far," Illegal Art, http://www.illegal-art.org.

54. "Grey Tuesday," Electronic Frontier Foundation.

55. Johnstone, *Underground Appeal*, 397–432.

56. Abramson, *Digital Sampling and the Recording Musician*, 1666–95.

57. Albini, "The Problem with Music."

58. "The David Bowie 'Reality' Mash-up Contest," BowieNet.

BIBLIOGRAPHY

GENERAL WORKS

Abramson, Christopher D. *Digital Sampling and the Recording Musician: A Proposal for Legislative Protection.* 74 NYU L. Rev. 1660, 1660–95 (1999).

Adorno, Theodor W. "On the Fetish Character in Music and the Regression of Listening." In *Essays on Music,* translated by Susan H. Gillespie, 288–317. Berkeley and Los Angeles: University of California Press, 2002.

Agawu, V. Kofi. *Playing with Signs: A Semiotic Interpretation of Classic Music.* Princeton: Princeton University Press, 1991.

Aikin, Jim. Review of "N.Y. Cutz." Posted on *East West Sounds* Web site. http://www.soundsonline.com/revTASCD-89.shtml (accessed May 22, 2004).

Albini, Steve. "The Problem with Music." Posted on Negativland's official Web site. http://www.negativland.com/albini.html (accessed June 12, 2004).

Baraka, Amiri (Leroy Jones). *Black Music.* New York: William Morrow, 1967.

Baraka, Amiri, and Amina Baraka. "The Phenomenon of Soul in African-American Music." In *The Music: Reflections on Jazz and Blues,* 269–75. New York: William Morrow, 1987.

Barnett, Kyle. "The Monster and the Mash-up: The New Bootlegs and the Recording Industry." Paper presented at the Popular Music and American Culture Conference, Center for American Music, University of Texas, Austin, TX, November 23, 2002.

Battersby, Christine. *Gender and Genius: Towards a Feminist Aesthetics.* Bloomington: Indiana University Press, 1989.

Baudrillard, Jean. *Simulacra and Simulation*. Translated by Sheila Faria
    Glaser. Ann Arbor: University of Michigan Press, 1994.

Benjamin, Walter. "The Work of Art in the Age of Mechanical Reproduc-
    tion." In *Illuminations*, edited by Hannah Arendt, translated by Harry
    Zohn, 217–51. New York: Schocken, 1989.

Béthune, Christian. *Le rap: une esthétique hors la loi*. Paris: Éditions Autre-
    ment, 1999.

Bettig, Ronald V. *Copyrighting Culture: The Political Economy of Intellectual
    Property*. Boulder: Westview, 1996.

Bogdanov, Vladimir, Chris Woodstra, Stephen Thomas Erlewine, and John
    Bush, eds. *All Music Guide to Electronica: The Definitive Guide to Elec-
    tronic Music*. San Francisco: Backbeat, 2001.

Bollier, David. *Brand Name Bullies: The Quest to Own and Control Culture*.
    Hoboken, NJ: John Wiley and Sons, 2005.

Boucher, Geoff. "A Musician Writes It, a Rapper Borrows It: A Swap or a
    Theft?" *Los Angeles Times*, September 21, 2002, F1.

Boyle, James. *Shamans, Software, and Spleens: Law and the Construction of
    the Information Society*. Cambridge: Harvard University Press, 1996.

Boynton, Robert S. "The Tyranny of Copyright?" *New York Times Magazine*,
    January 25, 2004, 40–45.

Brabec, Jeffrey, and Todd Brabec. *Music, Money, and Success: The Insider's
    Guide to Making Money in the Music Industry*. 3rd ed. New York: Schirmer,
    2002.

Brennan, Tim. "Off the Gangsta Tip: A Rap Appreciation, or Forgetting
    about Los Angeles." *Critical Inquiry* 20 (1994): 663–93.

Bridges, Mary. "Rip, Mix, and Burn: Lessig's Case for Building a Free Cul-
    ture." Posted on Berkman Center for Internet and Society Web site,
    February 18, 2004. http://cyber.law.harvard.edu/briefings/lessig (accessed
    May 21, 2004).

Chadha, Tina. "Mix This: Young South-Asians' Love-Hate Relationship
    with Hip-hop's New Indian Beats." *The Village Voice*, June 2003, 2–8.
    http://www.villagevoice.com/news/0327,chadha,45230,1.html/.

"Composer Pays for Piece of Silence." CNN.com, September 23, 2002,
    http://archives.cnn.com/2002/SHOWBIZ/Music/09/23/uk.silence/.

"Contractual Issues." Posted on the Recording Artists' Coalition's Web site.

http://www.recordingartistscoalition.com/issues_recordingcontracts.php
(accessed May 21, 2004).

Coombe, Rosemary. *The Cultural Life of Intellectual Properties: Authorship,
Appropriation, and the Law.* Durham: Duke University Press, 1998.

Cruger, Roberta. "The Mash-up Revolution." *Salon*, August 22, 2003. http://
archive.salon.com/ent/music/feature/2003/08/09/mashups_cruger/.

Dark, Jane. "Push in the Bush." *The Village Voice*, March 23, 1999, 75.

"The David Bowie 'Reality' Mash-up Contest." Posted on BowieNet Web
site. http://www.davidbowie.com/neverFollow/ (accessed May 24, 2004).

Demers, Joanna. "Sampling the 1970s in Hip-hop." *Popular Music* 22, no.1
(2003): 41–56.

Doss, Erika. *Elvis Culture: Fans, Faith, and Image.* Lawrence: University
Press of Kansas, 1999.

Douglass, Susan Upton, and Craig S. Mende. "Music Sampling: More than
Digital Theft?" *Copyright World* 82 (August 1998): 23–28.

Elflein, Dietmar. "From Krauts with Attitudes to Turks with Attitudes:
Some Aspects of Hip-hop History in Germany." *Popular Music* 17, no.
3 (October 1998): 255–65.

Emerson, Jim. Review of *Saturday Night Fever: The Original Movie Soundtrack.* http://www.amazon.com (accessed April 23, 2004).

"Eminem Sues Apple, MTV Over iTunes Ad." *USA Today.* http://www.usa
today.com/, February 24, 2004 (accessed December 20, 2004).

Erlmann, Veit. *African Stars: Studies in Black South African Performance.*
Chicago Studies in Ethnomusicology. Chicago: University of Chicago
Press, 1991.

Feld, Steven. "Notes on 'World Beat'." In *Music Grooves: Essays and Dia-
logues,* edited by Charles Keil and Steven Feld, 238–46. Chicago: University of Chicago Press, 1994.

Finell, Judith. *How a Musicologist Views Digital Sampling Issues.* 207 New
York L.J. 5 (1992).

Floyd, Samuel, Jr. *The Power of Black Music: Interpreting Its History from
Africa to the United States.* New York: Oxford University Press, 1995.

Foucault, Michel. "What Is an Author?" In *Language, Counter-memory,
Practice: Selected Essays and Interviews,* edited and translated by Don-
ald F. Bouchard, 118–33. Ithaca: Cornell University Press, 1977.

Frith, Simon. "Music and Morality." In *Music and Copyright*, edited by Simon Frith, 1–21. Edinburgh: Edinburgh University Press, 1993.

Gaines, Jane M. *Contested Culture: The Image, the Voice, and the Law.* Chapel Hill: University of North Carolina Press, 1991.

Gates, Henry Louis. *The Signifying Monkey: A Theory of African-American Literary Criticism.* New York: Oxford University Press, 1988.

Geller, Paul Edward. *Hiroshige vs. Van Gogh: Resolving the Dilemma of Copyright Scope in Remedying Infringement.* 46 J. Copyright Society of the U.S.A. 39 (1998).

Gendron, Bernard. *Between Montmartre and the Mudd Club: Popular Music and the Avant-Garde.* Chicago: University of Chicago Press, 2002.

George, Nelson. *Buppies, B-Boys, Baps, and Bohos: Notes on Post-soul Black Culture.* New York: HarperCollins, 1992.

———. *The Death of Rhythm and Blues.* New York: Pantheon, 1988.

———. *Hip-hop America.* New York: Viking Penguin, 1998.

Goldstein, Paul. *International Copyright: Principles, Law, and Practice.* Oxford: Oxford University Press, 2001.

Goodwin, Andrew. "Sample and Hold: Pop Music in the Digital Age of Reproduction." In *On Record: Rock, Pop, and the Written Word*, edited by Simon Frith and Andrew Goodwin, 258–73. New York: Pantheon, 1990.

Gordon, Steven R., and Charles J. Sanders. *When Parodies Use Musical Allusion to Copyrighted Works.* 205 New York L.J. 5 (1991).

Gracyk, Theodore. *Rhythm and Noise: An Aesthetics of Rock.* Durham: Duke University Press, 1996.

Greenman, Ben. "The Talk of the Town: Silence Is Beholden." *New Yorker* 78, no. 29 (September 30, 2002): 48.

"The Grey Album Story So Far." Posted on the Web site. http://www.illegal -art.org/audio/grey.html (accessed May 22, 2004).

"Grey Tuesday: A Quick Overview of the Legal Terrain." Posted on the Electronic Frontier Foundation Web site. http://www.eff.org/IP/grey_tuesday .php (accessed May 22, 2004).

Grigg, Chris. "Very Processed TeeVee." Posted on the East West Samples Web site. http://www.eastwestsamples.com (accessed February 20, 2004).

Guy, Nancy. "Trafficking in Taiwan Aboriginal Voices." In *Handle with Care:*

Ownership and Control of Ethnographic Materials, edited by Sjoerd R. Jaarsma, 195–209. Pittsburgh: University of Pittsburgh Press, 2002.

Hamm, Charles. *Putting Popular Music in Its Place*. New York: Cambridge University Press, 1995.

Harrington, Richard. "The Groove Robbers' Judgment: Order on 'Sampling' Songs May Be Rap Landmark." *Washington Post*, December 25, 1991, D1.

Harvey, David. *The Condition of Postmodernity*. Malden: Blackwell, 1990.

Hochman, Steve. "Judge Raps Practice of 'Sampling.'" *Los Angeles Times*, December 18, 1991, F1.

Hochman, Steve, and Chuck Philips. "Pop Eye." *Los Angeles Times*, September 13, 1992, 69.

Horncastle, F. W. "Plagiarism." *Quarterly Musical Magazine and Review* 4 (1822): 141–7.

Jameson, Fredric. *Postmodernism, or, The Cultural Logic of Late Capitalism*. Durham: Duke University Press, 1991.

"John Cage Silence, Out of Court!" Posted on Peters Edition Web site. http://www.edition-peters.com/composers/Index.htm#top (accessed October 18, 2003).

Johnstone, Chris. *Underground Appeal: A Sample of the Chronic Questions in Copyright Law Pertaining to the Transformative Use of Digital Music in a Civil Society*. 77 Southern California L. Rev. 397, 397–432 (2004).

Kaplan, Benjamin. *An Unhurried View of Copyright*. New York: Columbia University Press, 1966.

Kaufman, Gil. "Judge Rules Truth Hurts' Album Must Be Pulled or Stickered." Posted on VH1 Web site, February 4, 2003. http://www.vh1.com (accessed November 14, 2003).

Kempfert, Chad. "Negativland Climb the Highest Mountain." Posted on Alternative Music Web site, July 30, 2001. http://altmusic.about.com /library /weekly/aa073001.htm (accessed May 22, 2004).

King, Jonathan Z. "The Anatomy of a Jazz Recording." In *ASCAP Copyright Law Symposium, Nathan Burkan Memorial Competition*, No. 40, 277–329. New York: Columbia University Press, 1997.

Kivnick, Helen. *Where Is the Way? Song and Struggle in South Africa*. New York: Penguin, 1990.

Kramer, Lawrence. *Classical Music and Postmodern Knowledge.* Berkeley: University of California Press, 1995.

Krasilovsky, M. William, and Sidney Shemel. *This Business of Music: The Definitive Guide to the Music Industry.* 8th ed. New York: Billboard, 2000.

Lanza, Joseph. *Elevator Music: A Surreal History of Muzak, Easy-Listening, and Other Moodsong.* New York: St. Martin's, 1994.

Lawrence, Tim. *Love Saves the Day: A History of American Dance Music Culture, 1970–1979.* Durham: Duke University Press, 2003.

Leeds, Jeff. "Dispute over Sampling Fees Has George Clinton in a Legal Funk." *Los Angeles Times,* May 20, 2001, C1.

Lessig, Lawrence. *Free Culture: How Big Media Uses Technology and the Law to Lock Down Culture and Control Creativity.* New York: Penguin, 2004.

Lhamon, W. T. *Raising Cain: Blackface Performance from Jim Crow to Hip Hop.* Cambridge: Harvard University Press, 1998.

Lichtman, Irv. "Suit vs. Biz Markie Settled." *Billboard* 104, no. 2 (January 11, 1992): 80.

Lipsitz, George. *Dangerous Crossroads: Popular Music, Postmodernism, and the Poetics of Place.* London: Verso, 1994.

Littman, Jessica. *Digital Copyright.* New York: Prometheus, 2001.

Locke, John. "Of Property." In *The Second Treatise of Civil Government,*. chapter 5, section 27. http://www.constitution.org/jl/2ndtr05.htm (accessed June 9, 2004).

Lowe, Melanie. "Claiming Amadeus: Classical Feedback in American Media." *American Music* 20, no. 1 (2002): 102–19.

Makeen, Makeen Fouad. *Copyright in a Global Information Society: The Scope of Copyright Protection under International, US, UK, and French Law.* Studies in Law: Center for European Law, King's College, London. The Hague: Kluwer Law International, 2000.

Marcus, Jason H. *Don't Stop That Funky Beat: The Essentiality of Digital Sampling to Rap Music.* 13 Hastings Communications and Entertainment L.J. 767, 767–790 (1991).

Maultsby, Portia. "Beginnings of a Black Music Industry." In *Who's Who in Black Music,* edited by R. E. Rosenthal and Portia Maultsby. New Orleans: Edwards Printing, 1985.

McLeod, Kembrew. *Freedom of Expression®: Tales from the Dark Side of Intellectual Property.* New York: Doubleday, 2005.

———. "How Copyright Law Changed Hip Hop: An Interview with Public Enemy's Chuck D and Hank Shocklee." *Stay Free!* 20 (Fall 2002). http://www.stayfreemagazine.org/archives/20/public_enemy.html/ (accessed 12 June 2004).

———. *Owning Culture: Authorship, Ownership, and Intellectual Property Law.* New York: Peter Lang, 2001.

Meintjes, Louise. "Paul Simon's *Graceland*, South Africa, and the Mediation of Musical Meaning." *Ethnomusicology* 34, no. 1 (Winter 1990): 37–74.

Merges, Robert P., Peter S. Menell, and Mark A. Lemley. *Intellectual Property in the New Technology Age.* 3rd ed. New York: Aspen, 2003.

Middleton, Richard. "All Shook Up? Innovation and Continuity in Elvis Presley's Vocal Style." In *Elvis: Images and Fancies*, edited by Jac L. Tharpe, 151–61. Jackson: University of Mississippi Press, 1979.

Mikkelson, Barbara, and David P. Mikkelson. "Happy Birthday, We'll Sue." Posted on Urban Legends References Pages Web site. http://www.snopes.com/music/songs/birthday.htm (accessed May 21, 2004).

Miller, Chuck. "Dickie Goodman: We've Just Sighted the Shark Again! He's Coming Straight for Us!!" Posted on America Online user Web site. http://members.aol.com/boardwalk7/goodman/goodman.html (accessed May 12, 2004).

Miller, Paul (DJ Spooky). "Loops of Perception: Sampling, Memory, and the Semantic Web." *Horizon Zero* 8 (April/May 2003). http://www.horizonzero.ca/ (accessed May 14, 2004).

Mills, Sherylle. "Indigenous Music and the Law: An Analysis of National and International Legislation." *Yearbook for Traditional Music* 28 (1996): 57–86.

Mnookin, Robert H., and Lewis Kornhauser, *Bargaining in the Shadow of the Law: The Case of Divorce,.* 88 Yale L.J. 950 (1979).

Morgan, Fiona. "Copywrong." *The Independent Online*, November 26, 2003. http://www.indyweek.com/.

Moss, Corey. "*Grey Album* Producer Danger Mouse Explains How He Did It." *MTV*, March 11, 2004. http://www.mtv.com/news/articles/1485693/20040311/jay_z.jhtml/.

Murphy, John. "Jazz Improvisation: The Joy of Influence." *The Black Perspective in Music* 18, no. 1–2 (1990): 32–47.

Negativland. *Fair Use: The Story of the Letter U and the Numeral 2.* Concord: Seeland, 1995.

Newton, James. "An Open Letter from Musician James Newton." E-mail circulated among the public, September 17, 2002.

Oswald, John. "Plunderstanding Ecophonomics." In *Arcana: Musicians on Music,* edited by John Zorn, 9–17. New York: Granary, 1999.

Patry, William F. *The Fair Use Privilege in Copyright Law.* 2nd ed. Washington, DC: Bureau of National Affairs, 1995.

———. "The First Copyright Act." In *Copyright Law and Practice.* Washington: The Bureau of National Affairs, 2000. http://digital-law-online .info/patry (accessed November 14, 2003).

Pellman, Samuel. *An Introduction to the Creation of Electroacoustic Music.* Belmont: Wadsworth, 1994.

Peters, Erskine, ed. *Lyrics of the Afro-American Spiritual: A Documentary Collection.* Westport: Greenwood, 1993.

Prendergast, Mark. *The Ambient Century.* New York: Bloomsbury, 2000.

Reynolds, Simon. *Generation Ecstasy: Into the World of Techno and Rave Culture.* New York: Routledge, 1998.

Sanjek, Russell. *Pennies from Heaven: The American Popular Music Business in the Twentieth Century.* New York: Da Capo, 1996.

Sanjek, Russell, and David Sanjek. *American Popular Music Business in the Twentieth Century.* New York: Oxford University Press, 1991.

Schaeffer, Pierre. *De la musique concrète à la musique même.* Paris: Éditions Richard-Masse, 1977.

———. *À la recherche d'une musique concrète.* Paris: Éditions du Seuil, 1966.

Schoenberg, Arnold. "Folklorist Symphonies." In *Style and Idea,* edited by Leonard Stein, translated by Leo Black, 161–66. Berkeley: University of California Press, 1975.

Scott, Hugh Arthur. "Indebtedness in Music." *Musical Quarterly* 13 (1927): 497–509.

Sebald, W. G. *Austerlitz.* Translated by Anthea Bell. New York: Random House, 2001.

Shapiro, Peter, ed. *Modulations—A History of Electronic Music: Throbbing Words on Sound*. New York: Caipirinha, 2000.

"Silent Music Dispute Resolved." *BBC News*, September 23, 2002. http://news.bbc.co.uk.1/hi/.

Sloop, John, and Andrew Herman. "Negativland, Out-law Judgments, and the Politics of Cyberspace." In *Mapping the Beat: Popular Music and Contemporary Theory*, edited by Thomas Swiss, John Sloop, and Andrew Herman, 291–311. Malden, UK: Blackwell, 1998.

Small, Christopher. *Musicking: The Meanings of Performing and Listening*. Hanover: Wesleyan University Press, 1998.

Smith, Christopher Holmes. " 'I Don't Like to Dream about Getting Paid': Representations of Social Mobility and the Emergence of the Hip-hop Mogul." *Social Text* 21, no. 4 (2003): 69–97.

Snowden, Don. "Sampling: A Creative Tool or License to Steal?" *Los Angeles Times*, August 6, 1989, 61.

Soocher, Stan. *They Fought the Law: Rock Music Goes to Court*. New York: Schirmer, 1999.

"Statutory Mechanical Royalty Rates." The Harry Fox Agency, Inc. http://www.harryfox.com/ratecurrent.html (accessed May 21, 2004).

"The Stuntman." Posted on the Respect Copyrights Web site. http://www.respectcopyrights.org (accessed May 29, 2004).

Sutcliffe, Phil. "Oasis: The Interview," *Q*, February 1996. http://www.oasisnet.com/qnoel.htm (accessed February 1997).

Swedenberg, Ted. "Homies in the 'Hood: Rap's Commodification of Insubordination." *New Formations* 18 (Winter 1992): 53–66.

Taraska, Julie. "Sampling Remains Prevalent Despite Legal Uncertainties." *Billboard*, November 14, 1998.

Taylor, Timothy D. *Strange Sounds: Music, Technology, and Culture*. New York: Routledge, 2001.

Thornton, Sarah. *Club Cultures: Music, Media, and Subcultural Capital*. Hanover: Wesleyan University Press, 1996.

Tomlinson, Gary. "Cultural Dialogics and Jazz: A White Historian Signifies." In *Disciplining Music: Musicology and Its Canons*, edited by Katherine Bergeron and Philip Bohlman, 64–78. Chicago: University of Chicago Press, 1992.

"U2 Sample Clearance Leads to Miami Buzz for Musique." *Music Week*, April 7, 2001, 8.

Vaidhyanathan, Siva. *Copyrights and Copywrongs: The Rise of Intellectual Property and How It Threatens Creativity*. New York: New York University Press, 2001.

Von Sternberg, Constantin. "On Plagiarism." *Musical Quarterly*. 5 (1919): 390–97.

Walser, Rob. "Out of Notes: Signification, Interpretation, and the Problem of Miles Davis." *Musical Quarterly* 77, no. 2 (1993): 343–65.

Ward, Brian. *Just My Soul Responding: Rhythm and Blues, Black Consciousness, and Race Relations*. Berkeley and Los Angeles: University of California Press, 1998.

Watkins, Glenn. *Soundings: Music in the Twentieth Century*. New York: Schirmer, 1988.

Werde, Bill. "Could I Get That in Elvis, Please?" *New York Times*, November 23, 2003, national edition, sec. 2.

Willful Infringement: A Report from the Front Lines of the Real Culture Wars. DVD. Directed by Greg Hittelman. Fiat Lucre, 2003.

Zemp, Hugo. "The/An Ethnomusicologist and the Record Business." *Yearbook for Traditional Music* 28 (1996): 36–56.

LAWS AND LEGAL CASES

Laws and legal cases are in chronological order.

U.S. Congress. *Copyright Act of May 21, 1790*. 1st Cong., 2d sess. *U.S. Statutes at Large* 1 (1790): 124.

U.S. Congress. *Copyright Act of February 3, 1831*. 21st Cong., 2d sess. *U.S. Statutes at Large* 4 (1831): 436.

U.S. Congress. *Dramatic Compositions Copyright Act of August 18, 1856*. 34th Cong., 1st sess. *U.S. Statutes at Large* 11 (1856): 138.

U.S. Congress. *Act of January 6, 1897*. 44th Cong., 2d sess. *U.S. Statutes at Large* 29 (1897): 481.

White-Smith Music Publishing Co. v. Apollo Co., 209 U.S. 1 (1908).

Shapiro, Bernstein & Co. v. P. F. Collier & Son Co., 26 U.S.P.Q. 40 (S.D.N.Y. 1934).

Sinatra v. Goodyear Tire and Rubber Co., 435 F.2d 711 (1970).

U.S. Congress. *Sound Recording Act of 1971*. Public Law 92-140, 92d Cong., 1st sess. (October 15, 1971), *U.S. Statutes at Large* 85 (1971): 391.

U.S. Congress. *Copyright Act of 1976*. Public Law 94-553, 94th Cong., 2d sess. (October 19, 1976), *U.S. Statutes at Large* 90 (1976): 2541.

Midler v. Ford Motor Co., U.S. Dist. Lexis 14367 (C.D. Ca. 1987).

Midler v. Ford Motor Co., 849 F.2d 460 (9th Cir. 1988).

U.S. Congress. *Berne Convention Implementation Act of 1988*. Public Law 100-568, 100th Cong., 2d sess. (October 31, 1988): 2853.

Tin Pan Apple, Inc. v. Miller Brewing Co., 737 F. Supp. 826 (S.D.N.Y. 1990).

Acuff-Rose Music v. Campbell, 754 F. Supp. 1150 (M.D. Tenn. 1991).

Grand Upright Music v. Warner Brothers Records, 780 F. Supp. 182 (S.D.N.Y. 1991).

Waits v. Frito-Lay, 978 F.2d 1093 (9th Cir. 1991).

Acuff-Rose Music v. Campbell, 972 F.2d 1429 (6th Cir. 1992).

Boyd Jarvis v. A&M Records, 827 F. Supp. 282 (D.C. New Jersey 1992).

Campbell v. Acuff-Rose, 510 U.S. 569 (1994).

Tin Pan Apple, Inc. v. Miller Brewing Co., U.S. Dist. LEXIS 2178 (S.D.N.Y. 1994).

Tuff 'N' Rumble Management Inc. v. Profile Records, Inc., 42 U.S.P.Q. 2d 1398 (S.D.N.Y. 1997).

Williams v. Broadus, U.S. Dist. LEXIS 12894 (S.D.N.Y. 2001).

Bridgeport v. Dimension, 230 F. Supp. 2d 830 (M.D. Tenn. 2002).

Newton v. Diamond, 204 F. Supp. 2d 1244 (C.D. Cal. 2002).

Newton v. Diamond, 349 F.3d 591 (9th Cir. 2003).

Bridgeport v. Dimension, 383 F.3d 390 (6th Cir. 2004).

INDEX